MARKETING PERFORMANCE

MARKETING PERFORMANCE

HOW MARKETERS DRIVE PROFITABLE GROWTH

THOMAS BAUER
TJARK FREUNDT
JONATHAN GORDON
JESKO PERREY
DENNIS SPILLECKE

WILEY

This edition first published 2016
© 2016 McKinsey & Company, Inc.

Registered office
John Wiley & Sons Ltd, The Atrium, Southern Gate, Chichester, West Sussex, PO19 8SQ, United Kingdom

For details of our global editorial offices, for customer services and for information about how to apply for permission to reuse the copyright material in this book please see our website at www.wiley.com.

Wiley publishes in a variety of print and electronic formats and by print-on-demand. Some material included with standard print versions of this book may not be included in e-books or in print-on-demand. If this book refers to media such as a CD or DVD that is not included in the version you purchased, you may download this material at http://booksupport.wiley.com. For more information about Wiley products, visit www.wiley.com.

Designations used by companies to distinguish their products are often claimed as trademarks. All brand names and product names used in this book and on its cover are trade names, service marks, trademarks, or registered trademarks of their respective owners. The publisher and the book are not associated with any product or vendor mentioned in this book. None of the companies referenced within the book have endorsed the book.

Limit of Liability/Disclaimer of Warranty: While the publisher and author have used their best efforts in preparing this book, they make no representations or warranties with respect to the accuracy or completeness of the contents of this book and specifically disclaim any implied warranties of merchantability or fitness for a particular purpose. It is sold on the understanding that the publisher is not engaged in rendering professional services and neither the publisher nor the author shall be liable for damages arising herefrom. If professional advice or other expert assistance is required, the services of a competent professional should be sought.

Library of Congress Cataloging-in-Publication Data is available

A catalogue record for this book is available from the British Library.

ISBN 978-1-119-27833-7 (hbk)
ISBN 978-1-119-27829-0 (ebk) ISBN 978-1-119-27838-2 (ebk)

Cover design: Wiley

Set in 11/14.5pt HelveticaLTStd by Aptara Inc., New Delhi, India
Printed in Great Britain by TJ International Ltd, Padstow, Cornwall, UK

CONTENTS

How do I ensure excellence in execution?

How can I drive change and sustain impact?

INTRODUCTION: SMART MONEY

If your marketing department were publicly traded, would you buy a share? If the new campaign were a pay-TV channel, would you subscribe to it? If next year's media plan were a business proposition, would you invest in it? If you hesitate even for a split second – and we would not be surprised – this book is for you. To take its proper place among its fellow functions, marketing needs to evolve from a cost centre to a profit centre. As the CMO, or as an aspiring marketing leader, you don't want to ask the members of the board or the shareholders of your company for budget clearance. You want to present them with an investment opportunity. You don't want your marketing plan to be perceived as a necessary evil, but as a good business proposition. You want marketing to advance the performance of your company in predictable and sustainable ways. You rightfully aspire to generate returns on marketing investment, be it in terms of sales, profit, market share, or brand equity. Make it happen, and you will never have to justify a budgetary line item to the CFO again – or smile and listen patiently as your fellow executives praise a competitor's creative campaign, asking why you never come up with something as clever as that, despite the fortune you are spending on all those hot-shot agencies. Sounds tempting? Then read on.

This is not a textbook for students of marketing theory. There are more than enough of those already. This a performance handbook for marketing practitioners. With trademark clarity, McKinsey's Marvin Bower defined performance as follows: "By performance, I do not mean just profits. Rather, I mean achieving the goals and objectives of any type of organization in an effective and efficient manner, with profits being one measure of the success of a business firm. Responsible decision makers all seek to improve the performance of their organizations." In this spirit, we aspire to provide marketing executives with hands-on decision support across all major performance levers, from budgeting and mix optimization to vendor management and organization. In contrast, we will not explore the underlying theory in more detail than is necessary for the practical purposes of this book. If you want to know more, please refer to the more comprehensive discussion of many of the concepts presented here in *PowerBrands*, now in its third edition, and *Retail Marketing and Branding*, now in its second edition.

This is not even primarily a book about marketing. It is a book about return on investment, focused on how an ROI mindset will help you transform the marketing function into a profit centre. Our primary objective is to empower you to open up new areas of growth for your company. Of course we don't have all the answers. But we are confident that the success factors we have derived from our work with leading marketers will help you plan, measure, and optimize the contribution of the marketing function to corporate performance. We encourage you to initiate a conversation about strategic priorities, even if that is the last thing some executives expect from the CMO. Don't hesitate to take on the big issues: What, exactly, are our goals and objectives as a company? Top- or bottom-line growth? Market share or profit margins? Short-term sales or long-term loyalty? Defend the home turf or conquer new segments, categories, and territories? This book will help you explain to your fellow executives how their answers affect your decisions: Which investments do I focus on? What messages do I send to customers? Which marketing instruments take priority? What kinds of tools do I need?

This is not a scholarly treatise. You will find that this is a straightforward book, down to its clean-cut structure and accessible language. It reflects our belief that simple things can make a big difference, even in a complex world obsessed with ever more data, ever more elaborate algorithms, and ever more intricate processes. Complexity is the enemy of agility, a key asset in a changing environment. Big data and advanced analytics are not ends in themselves, but means to an end, and that end is better marketing performance. We advocate data-driven decision making not for its own sake, but because we are convinced that quantified metrics are indispensable complements of experience and common sense. We explore topics like systematic insight generation and advanced analytics not because they are fashionable, but because we have found that they help companies establish a culture of evidence-based performance management. This is also why we have included dozens of application examples and case studies from a wide range of industries and countries. These examples provide both proof of principle and inspiration for your own agenda.

This book is based on our experience as consultants to senior marketers worldwide. It is anchored, quite simply, by the things that work: concepts, tools, and success factors that we have helped develop and apply in our work with clients. In this book, we set out to help you advance marketing performance with every dollar you spend, every decision you make, every person you hire, every service provider you buy from, and every ad you put on the air. We are acutely aware that your time and resources are scarce, and that you cannot possibly pull all levers at once. To help you pick your battles, we have arranged our material along the lines of five fundamental questions about marketing performance, reflecting the decisions you face in your work as a marketing executive:

- How much should I invest?
- How should I shape my messages?
- How will I reach my target group?
- How do I ensure excellence in execution?
- How can I drive change and sustain impact?

See the overview in Exhibit I.1 for details. But don't mistake it for a to-do list. You can't check off sections, chapters, and success factors like items in a work plan. A marketer's work is never done. While you are in the process of sizing your budget, competitors will change the game by driving up their share of voice. While you are still busy optimizing your mix of instruments, media owners will come up with new vehicles and formats. While you are in the middle of negotiations with a vendor, new service providers and solutions will pop up. A Paris-based CMO sums it up as follows: "Marketing performance management is like painting the Eiffel Tower. Just when you think you are done, it's time to start all over again." So, if in doubt, go for speed

Business questions	Success factors	
Where to spend?	1	*Budget sizing:* Combine multiple lenses to right-size your marketing budget
	2	*Allocation:* Put your money where your strategy is
What to say?	3	*Insights:* Discover what really matters to consumers to sharpen your proposition
	4	*Storytelling:* Take a publisher's mindset and tell stories that cut through the clutter
How to connect?	5	*One currency:* Compare apples to apples as you make trade-offs between instruments
	6	*Science:* Apply advanced analytics to drive fact-based mix optimization
Which way to execute?	7	*Smart activation:* Trim the fat off key instruments to drive incremental benefit
	8	*Partners:* Build performance partnerships with marketing service providers
How to drive change?	9	*IT solutions:* Use marketing ROI decision support solutions to transform your company
	10	*Agility:* Infuse your organization with a return on investment mindset

Exhibit I.1 Test success factors for answering your top five business questions.

and simplicity rather than for the perfect programme that will take years to develop and may be outdated when it finally takes shape.

We encourage you to dive into these pages with an open mind, be bold enough to ask the big questions, start with small improvements, and scale up the things that work – for your company, your brand, and your department. Not all the topics we cover will be equally relevant for all readers, but we are confident that there is something here for everybody who is serious about marketing performance.

There is an ocean of opportunity between perfection and inaction. Even if the challenge seems daunting, doing something is bound to be better than doing nothing at all. In our work with many of the world's foremost marketing executives, we have found that pragmatic, ROI-minded CMOs are consistently successful at forging alliances with their peers, engaging the supervisory board, and transforming the marketing function for the greater good of their companies. We encourage you to take control of the return on marketing investment, let others know what you are doing, and invite them to join your cause. Before long, the smart money will be on you.

June 2016
Thomas Bauer, *Munich*
Tjark Freundt, *Hamburg*
Jonathan Gordon, *New York*
Jesko Perrey, *Düsseldorf*
Dennis Spillecke, *Cologne*

1 – BUDGET SIZING

Combine multiple lenses to right-size your marketing budget

Why does budget sizing matter?

How much should you spend on marketing? It's the biggest question of all, and yet many companies settle on an easy answer. Most years, they spend whatever they spent the previous year. If they make adjustments at all, these are often a function of overall company performance: if the company is prospering, the budget goes up – sometimes beyond what is necessary or effective. And in times of stagnation or decline, marketing budget cuts are as certain as death and taxes, even if reduced marketing support is the last thing a troubled company needs. This is because a lot of companies still define their marketing budget as a percentage of past sales. In effect, budget sizing is decoupled from business requirements. Budgeting inertia is further aggravated by the fact that many companies buy media many months – if not years – in advance.[1] If you are serious about turning the marketing function into a profit centre that contributes to the company's bottom line, put an end to these wasteful practices and introduce zero-based budgeting. First conceived in 1970 by Peter Pyhrr[2] – a controller at Texas Instruments at the time – zero-based budgeting is about "reviewing every dollar in the annual budget",[3] taking nothing for granted, and only signing off on budget positions that promise sufficient returns. Applied to marketing, this is nothing short of a paradigm shift – from a cost item to an investment opportunity.

The role of marketing is not a constant, nor is your mandate as the CMO. Markets change, and so does your company's competitive position. Even your brand profile and your business model are bound to evolve over time. Such changes need to be reflected in the size of the marketing budget. Consider, for example, the case of an insurance company that depends on frontline excellence. If sales force performance is lagging, you may have to intensify your marketing communication to drive short-term consumer pull while your peers in sales do their homework to fix the underlying issues. Now fast-forward five years into the future. Aggressive new market entrants have declared a price war, and your competitors are launching secondary brands to secure their share of the lower end of the market. In this new situation, you will want to invest in brand building to strengthen your brand, justify your price premium, and protect the profitability of your company.[4] Now fast-forward 20 years into the future. Your brand is the top dog, and you are the market leader. You are finally able to decrease the marketing budget and allocate funds to other functions without putting your business at risk.

Whatever happens, we encourage you to put an end to "budgeting as usual." The size of your budget should reflect your ambitions for future growth, rather than the past performance of the company. Start treating budgeting as a profitability driver and build your budget as an investment case rather than as a cost item.

How to drive marketing performance with fact-based budget sizing

A few years ago, an electronics retailer embarked on a radical experiment. For an entire month, the company cut its ad spend by 60 percent. It was a top-management decision, just to see what would happen. Revenues plummeted. Store managers felt betrayed by the corporate centre, and their motivation dropped to an all-time low. But while the experiment substantiates the direct sales impact of advertising, it doesn't say much about the appropriate budget level. Indeed, 40 percent of last year's budget may be too little, but how much is enough?

Cause-and-effect relationships between the marketing budget level and market success are notoriously difficult to establish. There are simply too many other influencing factors: the creative quality of your campaigns, your mix of marketing instruments (see Chapters 5 and 6), prices, promotions, distribution, weather, seasonality, consumer confidence, competitors, financial markets. In light of this complexity, no tool or algorithm can give you the right budget level at the push of a button.[5] Historic relations between cause and effect should not be the only driver of sizing decisions anyway. Your company's objectives for the future and your own perception of market dynamics are equally important. Instead, we propose a multi-lens approach to budgeting that is both systematic and pragmatic. It starts with transparency creation and moves on to combine three perspectives on overall budget size (Exhibit 1.1).[6]

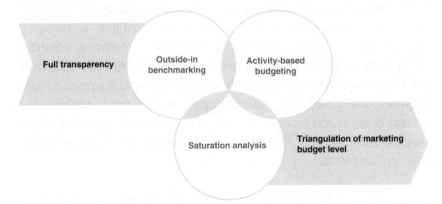

Exhibit 1.1　Five elements of budget sizing.
Source: McKinsey

Create full budget transparency; you will be surprised by what is hidden in the cracks and crevices of your organization

Transparency creation – it's easy to say and hard to do. This is because the marketing budget is scattered across so many different business units, functions, and departments at most companies. While most CMOs are in charge of all advertising, responsibility for activities such as co-op campaigns, sales support, public relations, owned media, and sponsorships often resides elsewhere in the organization. Yet all these activities affect your target audience in some way or another, and they should all contribute to your overall marketing objectives. A substantial share of the budget can also be hidden in the P&L of local subsidiaries, franchise partners, or affiliate companies.

So, before you even think about sizing, compile a comprehensive list of all the buckets in your current budget. Obviously, the number and granularity of budget positions will vary from company to company. Conceptually, taking stock should include all investments that are made to advance customers – current as well as prospective – towards your company on their purchase decision journey from awareness and consideration to purchase and loyalty. You don't need us to tell you that marketing is so much more than advertising. But in some industries – such as retail or B2B – traditional advertising typically only accounts for a relatively small share of the total budget. Make sure your transparency effort also captures point-of-sale activities, direct marketing, sales support, events, sponsorships, and indirect costs, such as agency fees and production expense. Compare our discussion of the "total cost of ownership" of a given touch point in Chapter 5.

The structures of most organizations – and the respective decision rules – are often the products of history and politics rather than business requirements. Typically, the marketing budget mirrors this internal view. As a result, the building blocks of the budget are often departments and business units, rather than products, channels, or target groups. But the budget should be a function of the market you are serving, the objectives you are pursuing, and the instruments you are using to reach these objectives. To promote an investor's mindset, we recommend you create transparency in two respects:

- Which objective is a given investment meant to support – brand building, customer acquisition, or sales support for a specific product or service?
- Which instrument, or combination of instruments, are we using to reach that objective in our target group?

This will lay the foundations for optimizing the allocation of funds to business units (see Chapter 2) and instruments (see Chapters 5 and 6). Ideally, investments should be split according to where and how they reach your audience: on TV, in a print ad, online, as a leaflet that is delivered to their homes, in a store, in the form of an addressed direct mailing, or as part of a loyalty programme. This will help you take on a consumer perspective, rather than worrying about budget ownership. Keep in mind that costs incurred at the same touch point may be split between multiple departments. For example, your company's website may be co-funded by the IT department, corporate PR, and your own function. Some marketing activities may not be treated as marketing expenditure at all. For example, co-funded sales stimulation campaigns are often managed as stand-alone profit centres. While this is good news from a return on investment perspective, it can turn transparency creation into a nightmare. Depending on the size and the complexity of your organization, transparency creation can take several weeks, but it is worth the effort. It will not only help you quantify the total "I" (investment) in "ROI" (return on investment), but often also triggers a productive debate among executives about appropriate allocation keys and accountability assignments.

Systematic transparency creation is imperative not only at the corporate level; it should be a matter of course for all your direct reports and their teams – be it to allocate funds to investment units (Chapter 2), to quantify the true cost of each touch point (Chapter 5), or to apply advanced analytics and optimize the mix of marketing instruments (Chapter 6). In each of these respects, transparency is the prerequisite of reliable, fact-based decision making. In this chapter, we will focus on the total size of the budget.

Outside-in: Conduct benchmarking analyses to find out what it takes for your voice to be heard

Your marketing activities don't take place in a void. You are in constant competition with other companies for customer attention. In a noisy environment, it isn't always easy to make sure your voice is heard. Of course, volume isn't the only way to get your audience to listen. A relevant message, a creative campaign, and a compelling story are equally important to engage your target group. But it's all for nothing if your messages never break through to them.

Marketing expenditure as a percentage of revenues is perhaps the most common indicator of relative marketing intensity. While this metric varies greatly with industry and country, it is a quick and easy way of determining whether you are spending in a healthy range. Typical ad-to-sales ratios range from 1 to 17 percent (Exhibit 1.2), but there is a wide spread within each industry.[7] In any case, you should have a good reason to spend either significantly below or above the average for your industry.

Of course, marketing as a percentage of sales is a highly aggregated figure, and it can easily be distorted. For example, if you are a B2B2C company selling to intermediaries, your ad-to-sales ratio will look disproportionately high. This is because sell-in to retailers is lower than sell-out to end customers. Because of such

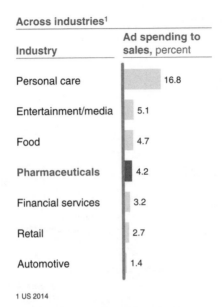

Across industries[1]

Industry	Ad spending to sales, percent
Personal care	16.8
Entertainment/media	5.1
Food	4.7
Pharmaceuticals	4.2
Financial services	3.2
Retail	2.7
Automotive	1.4

1 US 2014

Exhibit 1.2 Average ad-to-sales
ratios for different industries.
Source: Advertising Age, Capital IQ

distortions, you should use ad-to-sales ratios for rough orientation only. For benchmarking purposes, we recommend plotting your
share of spending (SoS) against your share of market (SoM).

The textbook opinion is that your share of spending[8] should
roughly match your market share to sustain your position relative
to competitors.[9] In general, our experience corroborates this rule of
thumb. But as the disguised example in Exhibit 1.3 shows, the "fair
share of advertising" is not normally a linear function of revenues. If
your market share is relatively low, you will have to overspend to get
noticed (Players 1 and 2). Conversely, if your market share is very
high, you are able to underspend (Player 3). This is a pattern we
observe consistently, across countries, various industries, and many
companies. Other reasons to deviate from the SoS/SoM equilib-
rium may be derived from specific strengths or weaknesses in sales
performance, brand equity, or promotion intensity. For example, a
high-performing sales force or a strong brand can compensate for

Share of spending (SoS)
Percent

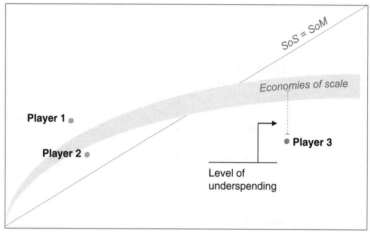

Share of market (SoM)
Percent

Exhibit 1.3 Outside-in benchmarking: Share of spending versus
share of market.
Source: McKinsey

part of the marketing communication investment that would normally
be required to reach a share of spending in line with your market
share. But if you are launching a new brand, or setting out to conquer a new market segment, you may need to overspend in relation
to your market share. In general, marketing communication should
always be managed as one of multiple interdependent commercial
levers, such as prices, promotions, brand, and sales.

When you conduct this kind of analysis, only include companies you
actually consider your competitors according to your definition of
the relevant market. Separate rounds of analysis may be required
for different countries and categories. Note that the share of spending in our example is limited to gross media expense, the only figure that is easily available in the public domain. For deeper insight,
the share of spending analysis should also include major below-the-
line positions – such as leaflets – especially for retailers. The trouble

is that this data is hard to come by, at least for competitors. Once you have gone through a transparency creation effort, you will know your own expenditure. There are different approaches to quantify the equivalent for competitors. Some providers of advertising data – such as AC Nielsen and Ebiquity – also track non-classical media. Alternatively, you can approximate below-the-line spending by deducting observed above-the-line spending from total marketing expenditure as given in a competitor's annual report. But keep in mind that reported ad spending is usually based on gross rate cards. In reality, most companies are awarded substantial discounts on those rates. A hundred "observed" advertising dollars might actually have cost the advertiser only 50 dollars or less in cash-out. Accounting for these rebates, which vary greatly across countries, is particularly important when you combine marketing spend data from multiple sources. We recommend that you conduct this type of analysis for the last three years to reflect the dynamics in the market. Typically, changes in SoM trail changes in SoS.

There is no wrong or right when it comes to your position in the SoS/SoM scatter plot. It's all about good reasons and conscious choices. If you are big enough or have other advantages over your competitors – such as a superior, patent-protected product or exclusive access to a key distribution channel – you may get away with underspending. Apple, for example, spends less than 1 percent of sales on advertising.[10] This is due to a combination of brand strength,[11] superior products, and lock-in effects that make it unappealing for many customers to even consider any other brand. From the perspective of many users, the perceived switching cost of transferring their music, photos, and contacts to another platform is simply too high to bother. Conversely, you may have to spend more than your fair share if your competitors have some such advantage over you. But be aware that focusing solely on SoS can lead to an unhealthy budgeting spiral that leaves all competitors worse off. This is why we encourage you to approach budget sizing from additional angles, namely inside-out and in terms of saturation effects.

Inside-out: Clarify your targets and build your budget on the activities required to reach them

The outside-in perspective afforded by competitive benchmarking is helpful to give you a sense of the right magnitude of your marketing budget. Your budget level should be high enough to get noticed in the marketplace, but it should also reflect what you are trying to achieve as a company. Because of the differences in marketing strategy and overall business objectives, benchmarking alone is insufficient to determine the appropriate budget level. The high variation we see both in ad-to-sales ratios and positions on the SoS/SoM scatter plot testify to the fact that companies differ in their growth ambitions, in their short-term versus long-term orientation, in the scale effects they benefit or suffer from, and in the operational marketing objectives they pursue.

Your budget should take into account both your general strategic direction and your market share targets. Building on these foundations, you can define specific activities and estimate the funds required for each. Ranked according to typical budget need in ascending order, examples include:

- Ongoing support for an established brand
- Launch of a new model or product range
- Organic growth with existing products
- Brand extension – to a new category, for example
- Introduction of a new brand.

Put yourself in the shoes of a consumer goods executive. Assume you have set out to build a new non-food brand for the Chinese market. Once you have outlined the structure and the size of your target group (e.g., all female consumers in big cities aged 19 to 45) and quantified your perception and preference targets (e.g., 50 percent aided brand awareness and 25 percent purchase consideration), your media agency can help you calculate the required reach and investment – for example, by using utility models as pioneered by von Neumann and Morgenstern.[12] Repeat this process for all the major marketing objectives you seek to achieve in a given year and sum up the individual investments to arrive at a total activity-based budget figure. To reduce complexity, you may want to go through this exercise brand by brand, country by country, or target segment by target segment, depending on the structure of your organization and the business priorities of your company.

In our experience, many companies will readily invest in highly visible above-the-line campaigns that drive awareness, but tend to neglect activities that drive purchase and loyalty. This is because such activities are often less spectacular than classical campaigns, and because they can be more cumbersome in terms of planning and steering. One consumer electronics company, for example, used to invest the bulk of their budget in classical media campaigns to promote their brand, partly spurred on by their creative agency that was desperate to win a Cannes Lion. But an analysis of consumer attitudes (see Chapter 3) revealed that lagging purchase consideration was actually the company's biggest issue. Subsequently, they included a range of activities in their marketing plan that would drive consideration, such as a new campaign featuring innovative products – rather than just the brand – and a set of activities targeting sales personnel at major electronics stores. In this case, the resulting budget was actually lower than before, but much more in tune with what the company needed to achieve in the marketplace to close the gap to its key competitor.

Saturation analysis: Review your budget in light of the expected return it will generate

Your competitors are going overboard with advertising spending. The noise they create calls for massive investments on your part as well, as do your ambitious growth targets for the company. And still it can be a bad idea to increase the marketing budget. Why? Because it may not pay off. Even if both outside-in benchmarking and inside-out activity planning lead you to believe a higher investment is required, the figure you arrive at may actually be beyond the efficient range. The disguised case in Exhibit 1.4 shows how the marginal ROI declines as the size of the budget increases.

As you can see from the shape of the curve, saturation is not a black-and-white affair. Long before your total budget reaches the saturation point, incremental returns generated by additional marketing investment begin to level off. In other words, your budget becomes less efficient the more you spend. As you get close to the tipping point, we encourage you to assess every new marketing activity, every additional instrument, and every request for a budget increase from one of your direct reports or product managers in light of the expected return. If your current budget already exceeds the saturation point, consider decreasing the budget to increase the relative return on marketing investment.

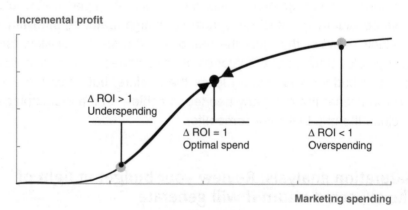

Exhibit 1.4 Saturation analysis.
Source: McKinsey

Additionally – or alternatively – you may also want to change the way you spend, based on this "marginal benefit" mindset. In this book, we will present a wide range of approaches you can apply to quantify and optimize the expected return on a given marketing instrument or activity. Granular growth analysis will help you find the investment units in which your budget is bound to have the biggest impact (Chapter 2). Insights derived from purchase funnel analysis will point you to the stages in a consumer's decision journey at which marketing investments are likely to be most worthwhile (Chapter 3). A common currency will help you compare different marketing instruments in light of their real reach per cost (Chapter 5). Creative storytelling is a great way to engage with consumers, often at very little cost because of the viral effects and free editorial coverage it generates (Chapter 4). Advanced analytical approaches let you optimize your mix across instruments (Chapter 6). Smart activation allows you to get the most out of your investments in specific instruments (Chapter 7). Don't hesitate to ask your trusted agencies for ROI estimates, and by all means have your team challenge their assumptions. Tying agency remuneration to marketing ROI can be a great way to motivate service providers to help you make your budget more efficient (Chapter 8). Screen the marketing technology landscape for solutions that enable you to monitor and manage marketing performance on a continuous basis (Chapter 9), and build an organization that is sufficiently agile and adaptive to react to relevant changes in market dynamics, competitor moves, instrument availability, and consumer behaviour (Chapter 10).

Combine all lenses for a holistic view on budget sizing and submit the result to practical, tactical, and strategic pressure tests

Each of the three perspectives described above – benchmarking, objective-based budgeting, and ROI analysis – will provide you with

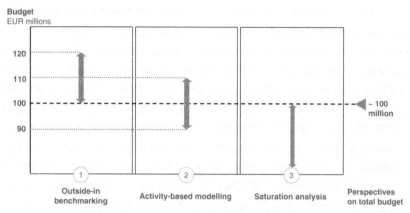

Exhibit 1.5 Triangulation of marketing budget level.
Source: McKinsey

a budget figure or, more commonly, a budget range. These ranges should show a fair amount of overlap. The company in our fictitious example (Exhibit 1.5) would have to spend EUR 90 to 120 million to achieve a share of spending in line with its market share and business objectives. But in the example, the saturation point for an ROI-positive investment is EUR 100 million. This is how much this company should spend.

Is that it? Not quite. The common ground defined by the combination of multiple budgeting lenses is only the starting point for real-life budget sizing. Before you actually submit your budget to the board for approval, you should perform a series of sanity checks and adjust the budget as needed:

- Have I considered all instruments? Make sure the three budgeting lenses have been applied to all marketing instruments. If you have missed out on any instruments, increase or reshuffle the budget accordingly. For example, your share of spending analysis may have been restricted to traditional advertising because of a lack of data for other instruments. Use objective-based planning to quantify other parts of the budget, such as below-the-line activities.

- Have I accounted for non-working spending? Activation is wasted unless you have something worth activating. Make sure you include sufficient funds for indirect cost in your budget, such as creative agency fees, production, licences, testing, and research.
- Can I turn to others for co-funding? If third parties share your marketing objectives, they may be willing to share the burden of your budget as well. As a retailer, turn to vendors. As a consumer goods company, turn to distribution partners. As a big spender, ask agencies and media owners for discounts.
- Have I taken discounts into consideration? Some analyses, such as outside-in benchmarking, are typically based on reported gross spending, rather than actual cash-out. You may be able to reduce the affected budget positions – such as ad buying – by whatever discounts your media agency – or the media owners you buy from – are prepared to grant you. Make sure you take a "net" perspective.
- Is the company ready for the new budget? Some changes may overtax the capabilities of your current organization. For example, running campaigns as profit centres might necessitate structural adjustments and require training for the managers in charge to succeed. Consider introducing changes to your budgeting approach step by step, rather than all at once.

When all that is said and done, lock yourself in a room with the brightest minds on your team and at your lead agencies. Have everyone come up with at least one idea for how to make your budget even more efficient. What about spending against the trend? Matching competitors' activities is often a very inefficient use of marketing funds. Companies that maintained their spending levels during the world financial crisis, for example, consistently outperformed their peers on the stock market.[13] Last but not least, make sure to set aside an emergency fund to react to unforeseen competitor moves, potential scandals, unexpected opportunities, and other surprises.

Budget sizing should neither be an automated process nor a black box. The systematic approach presented in this chapter is most powerful when you use it to initiate a fact-based discussion among your executive peers in other functions, brand owners, product managers, and country-level managers. Lay bare your reasons why, let them challenge your assumptions, and ask for their advice. If you have the big debate before the fact and make budget sizing a joint exercise, you will have a much stronger case against requests for midstream budget changes. And you will have your hands free for next year's budget planning.

Key takeaways

- Create full budget transparency. You will be surprised by what is hidden in the cracks and crevices of your organization.
- Outside-in: conduct benchmarking analyses to find out what it takes for your voice to be heard.
- Inside-out: clarify your targets and build your budget on the activities required to reach them.
- Saturation analysis: review your budget in light of the expected return it will generate.
- Combine all lenses for a holistic view of budget sizing and submit the result to practical, tactical, and strategic pressure tests.

NOTES

1. Jonathan Gordon and Jesko Perrey, "Boosting returns on marketing investment," *McKinsey Quarterly*, June 2005, http://www.mckinsey.com/insights/marketing_sales/boosting_returns_on_marketing_investment.
2. Peter A. Pyhrr, "Zero-base budgeting," *Harvard Business Review*, November/December 1970, Volume 48, Number 6, pp. 111–121.
3. Matt Fitzpatrick and Kyle Hawke, "The return of zero-base budgeting," *McKinsey Quarterly*, August 2015, http://www.mckinsey.com/insights/corporate_finance/the_return_of_zero-base_budgeting.

4. This is actually happening in many commoditized industries, from personal finance and airline travel to telecommunications and energy.
5. Advanced analytical approaches are required to control for external factors and isolate the business impact of marketing investments. See Chapter 6 for details.
6. The main section of this chapter is based on Tobias Karmann et al., "Budget sizing," pp. 117–128, in *Retail Marketing and Branding – A Definitive Guide to Maximizing Marketing ROI*, by Jesko Perrey and Dennis Spillecke, Second Edition, John Wiley & Sons, 2013.
7. Kate Maddox, "Capital IQ debuts first ad campaign," *Advertising Age*, October 20, 2008.
8. In an ideal world, you should measure and manage effective share of voice (i.e., the *output* that reaches your audience), rather than the share of spending (i.e., your *input* relative to that of your competitors). But in the real world, you will normally not have the data to quantify the share of voice you actually generate with your spending, except for a few instruments, such as TV.
9. John Philip Jones, "Ad spending: maintaining market share," *Harvard Business Review*, January/February 1990 (https://hbr.org/1990/01/ad-spending-maintaining-market-share).
10. YCharts, "Who spends more on ads—Apple or Microsoft? Another lesson in quality vs. quantity," *Forbes*, August 2, 2012, http://www.forbes.com/sites/ycharts/2012/08/02/who-spends-more-on-ads-apple-or-microsoft-another-lesson-in-quality-vs-quantity/.
11. According to Interbrand, Apple is the most valuable brand in the world, currently valued at USD 170 million http://interbrand.com/best-brands/best-global-brands/2015/ranking/ (retrieved 28 December 2015).
12. Glen L. Urban, "Direct assessment of consumer utility functions: von Neumann-Morgenstern utility theory applied to marketing," MIT Working Paper 843-76, January 1977.
13. Credit Suisse.

2 – ALLOCATION

Put your money where your strategy is

Why does budget allocation matter?

Let's talk about yogurt. Why? Because it's a booming business. Or is it? Between 2010 and 2013, the US yogurt market grew from USD 4.8 billion to USD 6.2 billion, an increase of 29 percent.[1] That made yogurt one of the fastest-growing non-durable categories in the US at the time. But when you take a closer look at the yogurt boom, you find that sales of regular yogurt were actually declining during the three-year period in question. The growth of the category as a whole was driven by a single subcategory: Greek yogurt. Greek yogurt sales increased more than fivefold, from USD 390 million to USD 2.6 billion (Exhibit 2.1). The bulk of that growth was generated in the Northeast of the US. What at first looked like a remarkable growth story turned out to be a story of widespread decline overcompensated by a local upsurge in a single subcategory. Additionally, a large part of the growth was not captured by any of the incumbent brands, but by Chobani, a start-up company operating out of the booming region.

This type of insight is often lost in the averages of national industry reports, to say nothing of international growth barometers. But a McKinsey study covering more than 800 companies over a period of 13 years reveals that the underlying momentum of a given market, category, or segment accounts for about two-thirds of an average company's growth. In contrast, capturing market share from

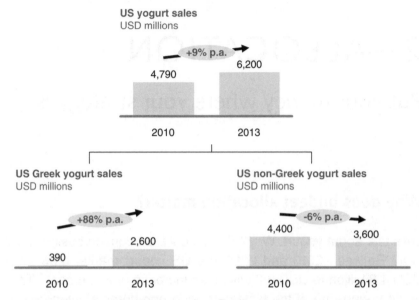

Exhibit 2.1   Greek versus non-Greek yogurt sales in the US.
Source: Nielsen

competitors only accounted for 4 percent of the growth for companies in our sample. So to stay competitive, you need to identify the growing business cells in your industry and prioritize your investments accordingly. In short, you need to de-average your business.

But while industry dynamics and market growth rates are subject to frequent changes, the marketing budgeting process of many companies is governed by inertia. In a separate study of more than 1,600 companies in the US, we found a very high correlation (0.92) between the budget a given business unit received in one year and how much it received the next. For one-third of the companies surveyed, the correlation was as high as 0.99.[2] These figures are the symptoms of deep-rooted corporate conservatism. When you talk to CMOs and CFOs about how they allocate their marketing budget to business units, two of the most frequent answers are "every business unit gets last year's budget +/- x" and "every business unit gets to spend y percent of last year's sales."

By default, these approaches preserve the status quo at the expense of growth cells that don't already have a substantial budget share or a track record of high revenues. Many companies end up overinvesting in areas that have played a large part in the company's history and supposedly define its identity, irrespective of current and future growth prospects. For example, a global passenger airline used to spend 60 percent of its worldwide marketing budget in its home market, a cluster of countries that accounted only for 40 percent of total sales at the time. What's more, sales in these countries were stagnating or declining. As a result, the company missed out on investing in growth opportunities in other countries, especially overseas. In another case, a beverage company invested almost its entire marketing budget in only a handful of its oldest and most popular brands. New brands in growing niche segments were underfunded and failed to reach their fair share of the market. This kind of allocation is often driven by corporate power play – essentially, executives defending existing budgets. In the case in question, the profit pools in niche areas were largely claimed by independent brands that received the full attention of their owners.

How to boost marketing performance with fact-based budgeting

To overcome the legacy effect of historic budgets and corporate politics, you need a fact-based allocation approach with sufficient granularity, clear decision rules, and the resolve to confront those who see their share of the budget as a sign of status and power, rather than as an investment in sources of future revenues and profit.

Find the pockets of growth

You want your fair share of granular growth? Then your marketing budget allocation approach has to reflect the granularity of what is happening in the market. This will help you reserve sufficient funds for growth opportunities as they arise and evolve. Start by defining the relevant splits: by country, category, business unit, brand, target segment, or a combination of these. Most companies either opt for a tiered approach – i.e., they define a hierarchy of multiple breakdown dimensions – or they work with predefined investment cells.

- A global car manufacturer allocates its marketing budget to brands in a first step, reflecting the roles of these brands in the corporate portfolio, such as "invest to grow", "sustain and harvest", or "phase out". In a second step, the respective brand budgets are subdivided by country.
- An international maker of consumer electronics has defined more than 300 investment cells, typically at the intersection of national markets and product categories. The cells are pricritized according to their potential and the budget is split accordingly.
- A consumer goods company works with three tiers of investment cells and allocates its marketing budget first to business units, then to national subsidiaries within these business units, and finally to regions.

For practical reasons, the primary breakdown should reflect the structure of your company. If the budget split is at odds with decision rights or P&L responsibilities, chaos will ensue. So if your company is structured by brands, the budget should be split by brands as well. The same goes for business units or product categories. Additional levels of division should reflect both organizational aspects and business opportunities in a given market, country, or category.

Once the general dimensions are defined, you need to specify the appropriate level of granularity for each. Take geography. You can work with clusters of countries, individual countries, additional splits by states or regions in a country, or even go down to the city level. Granularity should be governed by market dynamics, rather than corporate hierarchy. For example, marketing responsibility for a retail company may reside at the national level, but it will often make sense to differentiate marketing activities for regional clusters, if not cities or even neighbourhoods, for some budget positions, such as locally distributed leaflets.[3] Even companies with no regional infrastructure of their own may choose to promote different products in different regions.

More granularity brings more insight, but it also creates additional complexity in areas such as data gathering, budget management, and impact tracking. To find the right trade-off for your industry and company, examine how homogeneous the market is at different levels of granularity, e.g., in terms of average growth rates, competitive intensity, and your own growth ambitions. A European retail conglomerate, for example, opted for a highly granular approach to break free from an extended period of stagnation. In the past, the company had worked with about 200 geographic cells. But when they found out how big the differences were within these cells, they increased the resolution dramatically to more than 2 million cells that were defined using industry-specific criteria, such as average household income, basket size, and purchase frequency in various retail categories. The entire marketing budget was reallocated to the new micro-cells. Now the retailer was able to pursue growing, profitable parts of the market in a much more targeted way, using local media to support sales. The leaflet distribution budget was reduced, yet sales quickly picked up because the remaining budget had been reallocated to the most promising micro-cells.

Align allocation criteria with business priorities

Ask three board members how the budget should be allocated to investment units, and you will get four answers. The CEO, hoping to beat or even take over a competitor, is all for going by short-term revenue potential. The CFO, ever wary of how investors will react to the next quarterly report, will probably favour margin or EBIT. As the CMO, you may be inclined to go by the size of your target group in a given cell, or the strength of your brand relative to competitors. The fact of the matter is that these can all be valid criteria, depending on what your company is trying to achieve in the marketplace. The trick is to combine conflicting criteria in a meaningful manner, and to align the allocation key with business objectives and marketing opportunities.

Start by creating a long list of potential criteria (Exhibit 2.2). At this point, try to capture the perspective of all relevant stakeholders, even if that means that you end up with a list of 20 or 30 criteria initially. An inclusive, transparent process will help you mitigate political discussions during later stages. Make sure you include criteria from different categories:

- Financial criteria, such as revenues or gross profit, both current and expected.
- Strategic criteria, such as market growth or the strategic role of a category or market.
- Marketing criteria, such as share of voice or brand strength.

You can pressure-test the practical relevance of a given indicator by asking if and how it would affect the budget. For example, do high advertising prices in a given country call for a higher budget to put your national subsidiary on an even keel with those in other countries? Or should the budget be reduced and reallocated to other countries where advertising is more affordable? And does high brand strength justify higher investment to cash in on the strength, or should funds be diverted to other investment cells to compensate for relative weaknesses? This discussion will not only help you cross controversial criteria off your long list, it will also help you clarify what ultimately matters most to the company: top-line growth, profitability, market capitalization, or independence.

Don't use more than four to six criteria. More criteria will only bring marginally better results – if that – but they will add greatly to everyone's confusion and make it hard to explain the budgeting approach

	Potential criteria	Operationalization	Implementable?	Most relevant?	Non-correlated?
Financial performance	Revenues	**Business unit net revenues, 2015**	✓	✓	✓
	Historic revenue growth	Business unit net revenue growth, 2013 - 2015	✓	✗	
	Forecast revenue growth	Business unit net revenue growth, 2015 - 2016	✓	✗	
	Gross profit	**Business unit gross profit (net revenues – COGS), 2015**	✓	✓	✓
	Historic gross profit growth	Business unit gross profit growth, 2013 - 2015	✓	✗	
	Forecast gross profit growth	Business unit gross profit growth, 2015 - 2016	✓	✗	
	Business unit valuation	**Business unit valuation, derived from ISM analysis**	✓	✓	✓
	Business unit performance to plan	**Percent of performance to plan**	✓	✓	✓
Strategic priorities	Market share	Business unit market share within category, 2015	✓	✓	✗
	Market share growth	Market share growth, 2013 - 2015	✓	✗	
	Uncaptured market size	Net revenues of rest of market, 2015	✓	✓	✗
	Overall category growth	Net revenue/volume growth of total market, 2013 - 2015	✓	✗	
	Business unit strategic role	**Strategic prioritization**	✓	✓	✓
	Competitive intensity	**Industry advertising spend/market size, 2013 or SoV/SoM**	✓	✓	✓
	Brand/product innovation	Percent of expected revenues from innovation pipeline, 2014	✓	✓	✗
Marketing performance	Marketing cost factor	Cost of 30-minute TV commercial as proxy	✓	✓	✗
	Brand equity	Brand equity calculation	✗		
	Net promoter score	Brand experience and product experience metrics	✓	✓	✗
	Brand relevance	Qualitative assessment on brand relevance to consumers	✗		
	Article group and product range size	Number of article groups within BU, 2015	✓	✗	
	Halo effect	Qualitative assessment on spillover potential inflows/outflows to/from a BU	✗		

Exhibit 2.2 Example of selecting relevant allocation criteria (illustrative).
Source: McKinsey

to anyone who isn't an expert. To cut down your initial long list to the handful of criteria that really matter, apply four simple filters to each prospective criterion:

- Can you actually implement it? For example, do you have the required data at the level of granularity defined by your investment units?
- Is it really relevant to allocate the budget, i.e., will variance in the indicator call for variance in the budget?
- Is it sufficiently differentiating, i.e., do the investment units you have defined actually achieve significantly different scores?
- Is it independent of other criteria? For example, it doesn't make sense to use both market share based on volume (units sold) and market share based on value (revenues) because these criteria are highly correlated.

Consider the case of a consumer electronics company. The head of product development strongly advocated using the "number of products per business unit" as part of the allocation key, suggesting that a business unit managing more products than others should also receive more budget to support the products with marketing activities. While this indicator would have been easy to implement, it didn't pass the second filter. Because the company never ran more than five to ten product-related campaigns per year anyway, it would not make a difference whether a business unit oversees 50, 150, or 500 products. The criterion turned out to be irrelevant from a budget allocation perspective, although it may well have been relevant in other contexts, such as R&D funding.

A US telecom company pursued an even more sophisticated approach to narrow down their long list of criteria. Initially, the list included as many as 60 criteria. But instead of using the four filters, they tapped into the company's rich database and applied linear regression analysis to assess the relative influence of each criterion on key performance indicators, such as new customer acquisition, average revenue per user (ARPU), and customer retention rates. This allowed the company to prioritize allocation criteria based on actual business impact, rather than judgement. Eventually, the operator selected six criteria for budget allocation purposes, including market share, demographic composition, and network quality. Based on the new allocation logic, the company shifted about 30 percent of its marketing budget from large, saturated markets to smaller markets with greater growth opportunities. As a result, net customer acquisition increased by 3 percent.

To fine-tune the way the criteria influence budget allocation, individual criteria can be weighted to accommodate different strategic priorities for different regions, business units, brands, or periods in time. For example, assume your company has recently entered a new regional market and is building its business there. To account for this fact, you could attach double weight to "market growth" for that country. This will ensure that the country in question receives sufficient funds to support the company's growth expectations. And while the set of criteria should be maintained from year to year, weights can be adjusted as strategic priorities change.

Specify investment thresholds

According to the law of diminishing returns,[4] more funding doesn't necessarily create more growth, or only up to a point. Beyond that point, the incremental impact of additional investment decreases and eventually fades away. Conversely, any budget below a certain level may be ineffective, e.g., because your share of voice in a noisy environment is simply too low for your advertising to register with consumers. To reflect both of these effects and protect your company from wasteful spending, your allocation key should include investment thresholds. Common types of thresholds include:

- ROI-based thresholds below and above which the expected marginal effects strongly decrease (see Chapter 6 on how advanced analytics can help to determine ROI).

- Strategy-based thresholds to cap spending on lower-priority investment units (e.g., a maximum budget-to-sales ratio), or to prioritize specific markets (e.g., a minimum budget level for emerging markets or newly established categories).
- Capability-based thresholds to curb funds allocated to investment units with limited marketing capabilities. For example, a newly formed business unit may not be equipped to handle a multimillion dollar marketing budget effectively.
- Continuity-based thresholds to avoid disruptive change and let the organization adjust to higher or lower budget levels. For example, budget changes could be limited to +/- 20 percent of the budget received in the last planning period.
- Benchmark-based thresholds to ensure that marketing spending is in line with industry best practices, or that it reflects the share of voice required to break through the noise of competitive advertising intensity in a given market.

Many companies only look at marketing intensity in terms of advertising in classical media, primarily because this information is easily available from advertising tracking agencies. But using classical media budgets as proxies of total marketing spending can lead to serious distortions. For example, a company that invests primarily in sponsorships and branded events (compare the Red Bull case insert in Chapter 4) will be vastly underrepresented in this kind of analysis. To counter this effect, a global car manufacturer went to great lengths to collect meaningful benchmarks in more than a dozen priority markets, both for its own brands and those of key competitors. The company created a database of more than 4,000 sponsoring engagements and events financed by its competitors. A dedicated team broke down the cost drivers – such as licence fees and activation – to estimate the necessary investments, combining information from a variety of sources. Similarly meticulous approaches were applied to other unknown parts of competitors' marketing budgets, such as direct marketing, customer relationship management (CRM), and dealer marketing. Based on this effort, the company was able to set much more accurate investment thresholds, even for local below-the-line spending. The expanded fact base put an end to political discussions about individual line items in the marketing budget.

For details on how to allocate funds within a given investment cell – such as a national market or a product category – to specific marketing vehicles – such as classical advertising or direct marketing – see Chapters 5 (one currency) and 6 (advanced analytics).

Stick to the rules

With the investment units specified and the allocation criteria identified, you are ready to allocate the budget. A simple scoring model enables you to compare investment units according to your weighted allocation criteria, e.g., 20 percent past sales, 30 percent current margin, and 50 percent future market growth. Don't forget to apply the appropriate investment thresholds, including both minimum and maximum levels. These thresholds act as "reality adjustments" and help you reallocate excess budget recommended by the scoring model for a given cell (Exhibit 2.3), ideally to cells for which the recommended budget is below the minimally effective level. Don't allocate the entire budget though. Set aside an emergency fund to be able to react to changes in the market environment – such as a new regulation or an unexpected competitor move – or to try out new marketing instruments as they become available. See Exhibit 2.4 for a disguised example of fact-based budget allocation in the financial services industry.

Before submitting the new budget for board approval, make sure all relevant stakeholders understand and approve of the allocation approach. Of course, approval of the approach doesn't mean that everyone will be happy with the outcome. This is bound to happen and you shouldn't let anyone tamper with the criteria to change the results. This kind of interference undermines the whole idea of fact-based allocation and throw you back to endless arguments about

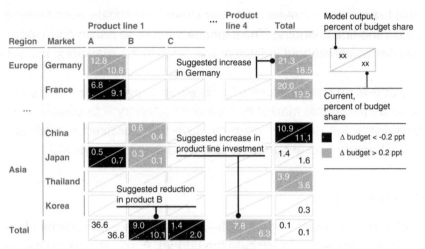

Exhibit 2.3 Example of allocation heatmap, percent of budget share.
Source: McKinsey

political and historical issues. Constant changes are also bound to frustrate your marketing team. Here is what a seasoned marketing executive told us: "After weeks of negotiations, I was informed that I would get EUR 50 million for the next year. It took me weeks to plan our marketing activities to make the most of these funds. But

		Factors considering business objectives							
		Strategic			Financial		Marketing		
Net sales account for 40% of weighting for budget allocation		Segment attrac- tiveness	Relative growth plan	Net sales	Profit contri- bution	Funnel perfor- mance	Competi- tive intensity		Allocation
		15	15	40	20	5	5	Current plan	model result
Category	Name								
Payments and transactions	Current account	17	58	55	29	9	46	41	42
	Bank card	22	15	9	18	24	11	16	15
	Term deposit	14	16	7	13	20	13	9	12
Financing	Consumer credit	6	6	6	17	19	7	8	9
	Mortgage	6	1	4	3	7	1	8	4
	Credit card	35	4	19	20	21	22	18	20

For its revenue share, 19% is coming from credit cards

Current plan is to spend 8% of marketing budget on mortgage product

Model allocates 4% of budget to mortgage

Exhibit 2.4 Example: Simple transparent overview of budget allocation.
Source: McKinsey

two months into the new year, my budget was cut by EUR 10 million, and my team spent another four weeks adjusting the plan for the rest of the year. Had I known right away that I would have only 40 million, I could have spared everyone hours and hours of overtime. Then, in late November, I got another 10 million because the company was doing well. But the condition was to use the additional funds that same year. I had no choice but to spend the money in December, when advertising cost is at an all-year high, and I get the least bang for the buck. By the end of that year, half my team was burnt out, and I was ready to chuck my job".

Don't let this happen to you. Dig as deep as you need to find the most promising pockets of growth for your company, define allocation criteria and weights that reflect your company's business priorities, adjust the recommended budget to make sure you are spending within efficient brackets, and stick to the rules. If you do, you will be well prepared to ride the next growth wave, be it foreign air travel, local retail, or Greek yogurt.

Application example: Sophisticated allocation in the automotive industry

A regional car manufacturer with global growth aspirations had traditionally allocated its marketing budget based on past sales volume. Experienced executives then often made adjustments to the allocation. To reflect future sources of value in its allocation, the company decided to implement a more systematic decision-making process. This was especially important as the company was about to expand to new markets with no sales track record that could have guided budget allocation to these cells.

As a first step, the company quantified future profit pools for all combinations of brands and countries, taking into account metrics such as market growth and competitive intensity. This calculation was further differentiated by time horizons: short term, medium term, and long term. In a second step, the resulting profit pools were discounted, using the weighted average cost of capital (WACC) for each cell to determine net present value. This was the basis for a first round of budget allocation. In a third step, adjustments were made to allocate extra budget to cells earmarked for many new launches or ambitious growth targets. Finally, the team conducted a round of sanity checks, using benchmarks such as the ratio of share of voice to share of market. This was to make sure that the spending in a given cell was neither too low to go unnoticed nor so high that it would exceed the corridor of sufficient marginal returns.

As a result of this systematic approach, about a quarter of the company's marketing budget was reallocated to improve the alignment of marketing pressure with business objectives. The CMO's team was lauded for adopting a wider business perspective, rather than the narrow marketing perspective that had governed previous rounds of negotiations.

Key takeaways

- Find the pockets of growth. Keep in mind that growth opportunities are often hidden in the average.
- Align allocation criteria with business priorities. Combine financial, strategic, and marketing-related perspectives.
- Specify investment thresholds to make sure your investment in each cell is within efficient spending ranges.
- Stick to the rules of fact-based allocation to overcome corporate inertia and avoid frustration in your team.

NOTES

1. Hamdi Ulukaya, "Chobani's founder on growing a start-up without outside investors," *Harvard Business Review*, October 2013.
2. Stephen Hall, Dan Lovallo, and Reiner Musters, "How to put your money where your strategy is," *McKinsey Quarterly*, March 2012.
3. Compare Thomas Bauer, Jan Middelhoff, "Leaflets and local print advertising: How to achieve local media excellence," pp. 217–230 in *Retail Marketing and Branding – A Definitive Guide to Maximizing Marketing ROI*, by Jesko Perrey and Dennis Spillecke, Second Edition, John Wiley & Sons, 2013.
4. Stanley L. Brue, "Retrospectives: The law of diminishing returns," *Journal of Economic Perspectives*, 1993, Volume 7, Number 3, pp. 185–192.

3 – INSIGHTS

Discover what really matters to consumers to sharpen your proposition

Why do insights matter?

You think you own your brand, but you don't. Customers do at least as much as you do. Their perception determines what your brand can do: the competitors it can outperform, the products it can support, the price premium it can generate. And because customers own your brand, you cannot afford to steer it inside-out, or at least not exclusively. No brand can be everything to all people. On the contrary. The sharper the profile of your brand, and the more differentiated its proposition, the bigger your chance is to stand out from the crowd. The flipside is that even a strong brand will wear out if it is spread too thin, be it by trying to compete in too many different categories, or by targeting too many different customer segments. So to maximize the value of your brand – and the return on your marketing investment – you need to understand what customers really want, to what extent they are getting it from your brand, and how you can keep them coming back for more.

You may think brand success is all about the media budget, but it isn't. Message beats media. Understanding what customers need will not only help you optimize the positioning of your brand, it will also enable you to send the right kind of messages – messages that resonate with your target audience and put your marketing dollars to good use. Even the biggest activation budget will evaporate if you don't use it to push the right buttons. In contrast, even a small budget can go a long way if you play your cards right. Think of old-school word of mouth, or of videos going viral in social media. Target group relevance and focused messaging become even more important as consumers are exposed to ever more advertising. City dwellers today see and hear an average of 5,000 brand messages every day – up from less than half that 30 years ago.[1] If you want to get anyone's attention in this noisy world, your message has to be both relevant and crystal clear.

To generate the fact base that will enable you to optimize your positioning and focus your messages, you need science. More precisely, what you need is a combination of quantitative market research and smart analytics that tell you what customers value, to what extent your brand delivers it, and which levers you can pull to improve your performance relative to your competitors. Using the positioning as your springboard, you will be able to devise the right messages and campaigns to get customers' attention and win their favour. Then, and only then, will your marketing dollars do what they are supposed to do: strengthen your brand and generate an optimal return for your business.

How to strengthen your brand with insights

You can apply science to marketing decision making in any number of ways. During decades of service to many of the world's strongest brands, we have identified six success factors when it comes to finding the right brand messages.

Slice and dice your audience: Customer segmentation

In most markets, different types of customers want different things, and they take different paths as they make up their minds about a purchase decision. Successful companies acknowledge these differences and inflect their messages to different customer groups, or segments, accordingly. Leading players manage an entire portfolio of brands, sometimes even in a single category, to reflect the diversity of needs and develop attractive propositions for different customer segments. The Volkswagen automotive group, for example, comprises close to a dozen brands, offering everything from versatile subcompact cars, such as the VW Up!, to luxury sedans, such as the Bentley Mulsanne. Other brands in the Volkswagen portfolio include Audi, Skoda, Seat, Lamborghini, Bugatti, Porsche, MAN, and Scania.

But even a single brand today cannot afford to be a monolith. In fact, the most successful brands actively seek differentiation within their lineup of ranges and product brands. Take BMW. The company has enjoyed four decades of success with its sporty M range, introduced the rugged X range in 1999, and most recently launched BMW i to bring the company's definition of driving pleasure into the electric age. But it doesn't stop there. One more level down, the product and model lineup has seen unprecedented differentiation in recent years to cater to the needs of a growing and ever more diverse audience. Previously, there were three model ranges, referred to at BMW as series: 3, 5, and 7. Now the numbers 1, 2, 4, and 6 have been claimed by BMW as well, each series with its value proposition and communication tailored to the respective target audience. The brand's overall range is impressive, from the sporty i8 hybrid to the 2 Series active tourer, a front-wheel drive family van. And we haven't even begun to talk about body styles.

So, successful companies differentiate their brand portfolios – both on the corporate and the product level – to serve different customer segments. In a similar spirit, every brand manager should make conscious choices about which customers to go after and which ones to stay away from. Then again, few companies like to leave substantial profit pools untapped. If an attractive customer segment is too far away from your main brand in terms of needs, it might be worth pursuing it with a second brand. This is a strategy that many players in the mobile telecoms industry have chosen, both in highly saturated markets, such as the Netherlands, and in emerging markets with very different customer types, such as some Middle Eastern countries. See the insert below for an example.

Application example: Fact-based customer targeting in the telco industry

Let's look at an example to illustrate how insights-driven market segmentation can shape the marketing mix, enable competitive differentiation, and create value for companies. A telecom operator – formerly the state-owned monopolist – faced increasing competition in a deregulated market that was forecast to grow very slowly over the course of the next five years. Most recently, the government had authorized the establishment of mobile virtual network operators (MVNOs) that were expected to increase competition for mobile users dramatically. To make things worse, the company's standing was already weak in some demographic segments. While the company was the first choice for the majority of the adult population, only about one in three younger users had committed to the brand as their main provider. The marketing department, however, was unclear about the root causes behind this relative weakness among younger users.

To get to the bottom of this issue and prepare the company for the imminent increase in competition, the company decided to conduct a segmentation effort based on user attitudes in areas including communications, entertainment, and lifestyle, rather than just based on demographics. Using statements such as "I am willing to pay more for a well-established brand", "I need to get access to the Internet everywhere", or "I prefer a brand that is for young, modern, fashionable people", three main target groups were identified:

- *Affluent locals.* These users have an above-average income, low price sensitivity, and care a lot about the latest handset as a lifestyle accessory.
- *Smart onliners.* These young locals are constantly looking for the best deal to accommodate their heavy data traffic at reasonable prices.
- *Pragmatic professionals.* Most of these customers travel frequently, but they only use basic telephony. They are extremely price sensitive, especially regarding roaming fees.

While the company's existing positioning and product portfolio was closest to the needs of pragmatic professionals, their value propositions to the other two target segments were less pronounced. In response to these findings, the company took triple action:

- Fine-tune roaming costs for pragmatic professionals. The option to pay a moderate monthly fee to get a substantial discount on all international calls was introduced.
- Introduce new services for smart onliners. Tailor-made products were created, e.g., subscriptions to preferred types of content, such as music or games.
- Launch new brand for affluent locals. To provide the exclusivity valued by these users, the company is preparing to launch a second fully differentiated brand.

Ever since these actions took effect, the company has seen a rapid rise in new postpaid contracts, fewer contract cancellation requests, and less migration from postpaid to prepaid rate structures.

Segmentation is not only a rewarding exercise in its own right, it also serves as a lever to increase the effectiveness of the other success factors discussed in this chapter. While they are all valuable in themselves, each and every one of them is more powerful if applied on a segment level, rather than to the market as a whole. Insights generated for a specific segment will typically be more concrete and take you closer to the actions you can take to improve the performance of your brand. We recommend including a segmentation module in all your brand surveys, both for exploratory purposes and to track brand performance or advertising effectiveness over time. Such modules are typically operationalized as a set of questions covering demographics (e.g., age), sociographics (e.g., income), and psychographics (e.g., values and attitudes). The answers to these questions can be used to derive and monitor clusters of customers with similar needs.

Put your brand to the test: Purchase funnel performance

Some sales agents are great at attracting attention, while others are more effective when it comes to closing a deal. Brands are no different. To find out what your brand is like, you need to compare its performance with competitors throughout the brand purchase funnel: What percentage of your target group is aware of the fact that your brand exists? How many of them would consider buying one of your products? And once they have bought from you, how likely are they to do it again, or to recommend your brand to their friends? What are the brand's strengths and weaknesses in the purchase

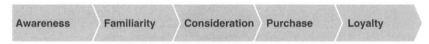

Exhibit 3.1 Simplified brand purchase funnel.
Source: McKinsey

funnel? Maybe your brand is considered by a lot of people, but many of those who consider it end up choosing another brand. That other brand may generate less consideration, but succeed at converting a higher percentage of those who consider it into actually buying one of its products. This kind of research will give you a good sense of how your brand performs relative to its competitors, and where there are bottlenecks that call for your action. Zooming in on the biggest gaps will make sure you spend your time and money where they will have the biggest impact on brand success. Purchase funnel analysis also is crucial homework to find out what customers are getting from your competitors that they are not getting from you.

Different frameworks are available to measure a brand's performance to model a customer's decision process. While the classic brand purchase funnel (Exhibit 3.1) is linear, assuming that consumers move from one stage to the next consecutively, the decision journey framework (Exhibit 3.2) acknowledges that customers may go back and forth between stages and touch points, or add new brands at later stages. The funnel is well established and widely applied across markets and categories. It is well suited both to quick diagnostics and long-term tracking of brand performance over time. In contrast, decision journey analysis allows companies to capture a more dynamic decision-making process, as well as to examine specific high-impact touch points in greater detail than others. McKinsey pioneered a range of proven solutions in either area, from BrandMatics (classic funnel) to CDJ (customer decision journey[2]) and BrandMatics 2.0, a recent module that incorporates dynamic elements – such as impulse decisions – into the classic funnel.[3] We encourage you to take your time to determine which framework best

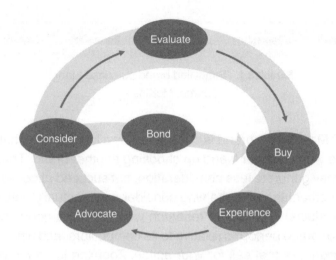

Exhibit 3.2 Consumer decision journey.
Source: McKinsey

reflects the decision-making process in your industry, and which tool best caters to your needs as a brand or marketing manager.

As you look at the output of any one of these methods, go beyond absolute values (such as "21 percent of all customers buy my brand") and look at the conversion rate from one stage to the next (e.g., "half of those who consider my brand end up buying it"). This will even out differences in size or current market share and get you closer to the kinds of insights that are relevant for your brand management decisions. For example, luxury brands will always have lower purchase rates than mass market brands, simply because the size of the target market is much smaller. However, even a luxury brand will rightly be keen to compare its conversion rate from consideration to purchase with its direct competitors.

Find out what customers want: Attribute relevance

You may think you know what your customers want. Do you really? Then why are so many of them are still buying from your competitors? Get ready to be surprised by what customer insights can tell you about why people behave the way they do. Done right, brand research will reveal the root causes behind customer decisions, causes that even they themselves are sometimes not aware of. Imagine for a minute you are the CMO for a major insurance company. Pretty much everybody knows your brand. In fact, your brand might well be the first one that comes to mind when you ask people to name an insurance company in many of the markets in which you compete. Assume that your main competitor, although slightly less well known, is more successful at converting customers from consideration to purchase in the brand purchase funnel. To take action, you need to understand what really matters to customers when they are about to choose a policy. To put it in technical terms, you need to find out which brand attributes drive the purchase decision.

A major European insurance company used BrandMatics research to determine these purchase drivers in the health insurance category and found that they differed by type of customer, validating their assumption that any improvements should be devised and implemented at the segment level. While prospective policyholders who had children were keen on family benefits, best agers who lived alone typically made their decision based on whether a given company pays for innovative or unconventional treatment methods.

Typically, only a few attributes really matter, and their relevance differs greatly depending on which stage of the funnel you look at. While dumping prices may be great to attract initial attention, building long-term loyalty requires strengths in areas such as product reliability and superior service. Even today, some companies are wasting millions by talking about attributes that don't contribute to what they are trying to achieve in the marketplace. Take the example of a major US retailer. Hoping to drive loyalty, the company ran a nationwide campaign promoting its loyalty card and the associated benefits, such as free meals at in-store restaurants. The effect was close to zero. To find out what had gone wrong, the retailer invested a fraction of the campaign's cost to determine the actual loyalty drivers in their market. It turned out that "has a loyalty card with good rewards" was at the bottom of the list. Rather, loyalty was mainly driven by two by attributes: "the store I trust the most" and "my preferred store to give myself a treat". Based on this insight, the company devised a new campaign revolving around trust and indulgence, a step that helped them close the loyalty gap to their main competitor.

To apply this kind of analysis to your industry, it is crucial to feed the right set of attributes into your survey design. Keep in mind that the list should not only reflect the profile of your own brand, but also attributes other brands use to differentiate themselves in your competitive arena. This is to make sure you capture the dynamics of the market as a whole. However, the total number of attributes respondents can meaningfully assess is limited. Some say you should keep the list down to 20, others will let you include up to 40 items. In any case, every slot in the questionnaire is quite valuable. We recommend that you use your own experience, existing research, qualitative studies, and the elements contained in your own and your competitors' value proposition to shape your list of attributes. Make sure to include functional attributes, like "long-lasting", as well as symbolic attributes, like "prestigious". While certain industries, such as personal finance or detergent, are primarily driven by rational factors, others, such as apparel or personal care, are more dependent on creating symbolic value. That said, some brands also succeed by zigging when others zag, e.g., by making insurance fun (think Geico), or by taking emotion out of the equation altogether (think Muji).

Also, keep in mind that customers will deceive you – be it deliberately or unknowingly – when you ask them directly about their preferences. For example, if you ask car buyers what they value in a car, many of them will quote fuel efficiency, good safety ratings, or value for money. But when you observe how they actually arrive at their purchase decisions, it becomes apparent that design, handling, and trendiness are actually much more important. Many ascribe this distortion to our inclination to say what is considered socially desirable in surveys. To correct for this effect, you should use derived importance, rather than stated importance, in your attribute relevance research. In practice, this means submitting actual behaviour to advanced analysis to uncover the driving forces behind consumer behaviour.[4]

Take stock of your strengths and weaknesses: Attribute performance

You think you know what your brand is really good at, and you have the test results to prove it. We hate to break it to you, but your target customers might disagree. Let's return to our insurance example. After consulting with the CFO, you have decided to go after affluent best agers because of their high customer lifetime value. Since they are already familiar with your brand and consider buying one of your plans, you need to understand what makes so many of them pick your competitor over you. You have previously determined that they value coverage of innovative treatments, such as homeopathy, and that they consider your company inferior to others in this respect. But when you look at the actual insurance plans, you find that your company actually pays for a wider range of treatments than your key competitor. Objectively, you are outperforming the other company, and still you can't get people to pick your brand. What you have is a perception problem, not an actual gap in terms of benefits provided. Of course, this effect can also work in your favour. Many US motorcycle companies, for example, don't achieve the level of their Japanese peers in reliability surveys. Yet American brands are widely regarded as makers of high-quality bikes anyway.

Ultimately, what counts is how customers see your brand, even if this perception is sometimes at odds with the sober facts. However, an assessment of the objective situation is crucial to develop a robust action plan. If you try to play a card you don't actually hold, chances are that you will eventually disappoint your customers. For example, a consumer bank that ran a "worry-free service" campaign long before their staff had been properly trained to deliver on that promise paid a high price for their haste. Attracted by the campaign, customers flocked to the bank's branches. Appalled by cumbersome processes, complicated forms, and unhelpful employees, they were driven away to competitors.

In other words, if you are already good at something that matters, but people just don't know about it, you might fix the gap in perception by way of communication – by talking about it more, or in other media than before, or in ways that make a given attribute more tangible to your target audience. But if you have an actual performance gap in a relevant dimension, such as shorter battery life than your competitor, or higher maintenance cost, don't talk about it before you have fixed the underlying issue. If you deny an actual weakness, or claim a strength you don't really have, customers will stop trusting your brand. To create a quick overview of the biggest opportunities, as well as of potential pitfalls, rank the brand attributes according to their relevance and map the performance of your brand against its key competitor; see Exhibit 3.3 for an example.

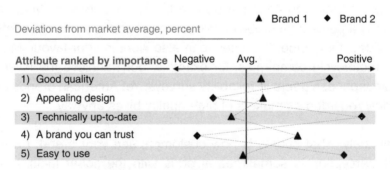

Exhibit 3.3 Attribute performance.
Source: McKinsey consumer survey

Map out your options and make a plan: Positioning and messaging

The potential to generate insight is infinite, but in real life you have to pick your battles. There might be any number of opportunities to improve the performance of your brand through fact-based repositioning, but you have to go after the most promising options. If you try to tackle too many issues in parallel, you risk overtaxing your team, running out of budget midstream, and confusing customers, none of which you can afford to do. So, to prioritize your actions, we recommend that you synthesize your findings into what we refer to as the matrix of options. Use one axis to plot attribute relevance in the context of a given decision and the other for the performance of your brand on that particular attribute. See Exhibit 3.4 for a disguised example of such a matrix.

- Top right: This is what your brand is really good at and what matters to customers. Build your positioning on these attributes.

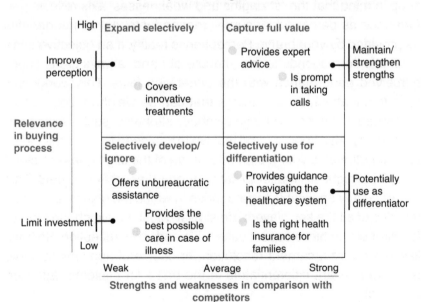

Exhibit 3.4 Brand attribute relevance versus performance matrix (healthcare example).
Source: McKinsey

- Top left: These are things that customers really want, but that you don't give them. Try to get your brand at least to market average on these attributes.
- Bottom right: You are good at this, but people don't really care much. Only invest in these attributes if they help differentiate your brand from competitors.
- Bottom left: These attributes are neither particularly relevant, nor do you perform particularly well on them. Don't waste your time with these.

In the insurance example, the decision in question would be "purchase of a health insurance plan", one of the highly relevant attributes would be "coverage of innovative treatments", and the perceived performance of your brand would be "below average".

While you contemplate your moves based on the matrix of options, keep in mind that the "strengths and weaknesses" axis reflects performance as perceived by survey respondents, not actual benefits as provided by your brand. Perception is reality. If an objective characteristic corresponds to the attribute at hand, always cross-check perceived performance with the underlying facts. This works well for rational attributes, i.e., things that can be weighed, counted, or measured, but not so well with symbolic attributes, such as image or personality. Also keep in mind that while you need to make the highly relevant attributes your top priority, some of the slightly less relevant attributes might still matter to set your brand apart from others. This is particularly applicable to categories in which the objective characteristics of all the key players are similar. Most mobile phones today, for example, achieve decent battery life and voice reception. So traits like screen size, camera resolution, or choice of apps might serve as more relevant differentiators in the battle for customer attention and loyalty.

Some companies choose to boil their positioning down to a short statement that is often referred to as the "brand promise" or "brand essence." Examples include BMW's "sheer driving pleasure," Nivea's "gentle skin and beauty care," or Sixt's "rental cars at affordable prices." This promise can be used both to align employees and as the starting point for creative agencies to translate the positioning into messages and campaigns.

Keep track of your brand: Checks and balances

It's never wrong to hope for the best, but it's even better to have the facts to prove you got it right. To check whether your insights-based positioning work is paying off, enlist the services of a research agency to update your framework of choice on a regular basis. This will tell you whether your actions are taking effect, help you quantify the return on your investment, and highlight areas that deserve further attention. Keep in mind that consumer needs will evolve over time, and that your competitors may try to reshape the market by changing or refining their propositions as well. For example, makers of consumer electronics who missed the trend towards mobile, wireless devices now find themselves out of business. Those, however, who understood that ease of use and versatility have gradually become more important to consumers than ever more features are reaping disproportionate rewards today. Frequent updates of brand attribute research can alert brand managers to such developments and enable them to take timely action.

While best practices vary with industry and market environment, we recommend updating brand performance research every 6 to 12 months to help you adjust your marketing messages. Complement these updates with more flexible tracking of social media and online buzz, potentially in real time. You may want to take advantage of a software solution, ideally hot-linked to your market research database. See Chapter 9 for details on IT tools, such as the BrandNavigator. Once every few years, you should invest in a more thorough analysis of your overall brand positioning to check whether it still reflects the needs of the marketplace.

Key takeaways

- Slice and dice your audience. Select and describe your target customers with care; needs and brand perception often differ widely between customer groups.
- Put your brand to the test. Pick the right framework to model customer behaviour in your industry and determine how your brand performs relative to its competitors.
- Find out what customers want. Observe how customers make decisions; remember that what they say they value is not necessarily what really drives their behaviour.
- Take stock of your strengths and weaknesses. Determine if you are giving customers what they really want; keep in mind that their perception may be at odds with the facts.
- Map out your options and make a plan. Build your brand and its messages on the attributes that matter most to your target audience; only promise what you can deliver.
- Keep track of your brand. Design your research updates to inform your decisions, both for ongoing marketing operations and occasional positioning reviews.

NOTES

1. Louise Story, "Anywhere the eye can see, it's likely to see an ad," *New York Times*, January 15, 2007, http://www.nytimes.com/2007/01/15/business/media/15everywhere.html.
2. David Court, Dave Elzinga, Susan Mulder, and Ole Jørgen Vetvik, "The consumer decision journey," *McKinsey Quarterly*, June 2009.
3. For details on these frameworks, please see the brand measurement section in *Power Brands*, by Jesko Perrey, Dennis Spillecke, and Tjark Freundt, Third Edition, Wiley, 2015.
4. For details on derived importance, see the discussion of brand drivers in *Power Brands*, by Jesko Perrey, Dennis Spillecke, and Tjark Freundt, Third Edition, Wiley, 2015.

4 – STORYTELLING

Take a publisher's mindset and tell stories that cut through the clutter

Why does storytelling matter?

It all started in Rushville Center, population 4,000. This is where Ma Perkins ran her lumberyard and raised her three children: Evey, Fay, and John. Ma Perkins was the title character in NBC's longest-running radio drama. First broadcast in 1933, it stayed on the air for 27 years. The show was scripted by Robert "Bob" Hardy Andrews, a singularly prolific writer who is said to have churned out 100,000 words per week on average. In his prime, he wrote the scripts for seven daily radio shows at the same time. He worked from noon to midnight every day, fuelled by five packs of cigarettes and 40 cups of coffee.[1]

Got your attention? Behold the power of storytelling. Telling stories is what this chapter is all about, and we didn't pick *Ma Perkins* at random. Sponsored by Oxydol, a former Procter & Gamble detergent brand, it is widely regarded as the world's first soap opera. Bob Andrews got listeners hooked by telling stories they could relate to, and *Ma Perkins* may well be P&G's most successful consumer engagement platform of all time. The show ran five days a week and mentioned Oxydol's name up to 25 times in each episode. P&G received 5,000 letters complaining about the aggressive product placement. But when they were offered a reward for proof of an

Oxydol purchase, listeners mailed more than a million box tops to P&G. By the end of the show's first year on the air, Oxydol sales had doubled. When P&G pulled out in 1956, *Ma Perkins* had helped the company sell more than three billion units of Oxydol.[2]

Storytelling may not be breaking news, but it is a vital tool for brands hoping to break through to consumers in today's era of information overload. The number of TV stations has increased fivefold since 1995.[3] On average, 189 channels are available to households in the US,[4] but more and more people are tuning out.[5] Online, more than a billion websites compete for user attention. Marketers everywhere have to work harder than ever to get and sustain the attention of consumers. Every day, 500,000 videos are uploaded to YouTube, and 500 million tweets are posted on Twitter. Storytelling is a way for brands to cut through this clutter, and it carries across multiple channels and media, an important asset in the omnichannel world. Why do stories have that power to attract and hold attention much more than traditional advertising? Because stories appeal to emotion as much as they appeal to reason. Long-form stories – regardless of whether they are told in videos or in written text – can deliver a far wider range of information and emotion than a simple print ad or a short TV commercial. This emotive quality of storytelling binds customers to a brand, and it keeps them engaged on a wide variety of devices and platforms. Brand stories drive word of mouth, the most powerful touch point of all.

So can any one story be all things to all people? Not likely. But the good news is that a brand can come to life in more than one story. While your brand should only have one identity and one promise, you can tell many stories to flesh out that promise for a diverse audience. As product portfolios grow[6] and consumer needs diversify, being able to deliver tailored messages to different target groups is a source of competitive advantage. By telling stories, the same brand can cater to a considerable variety of needs without compromising any of its identity.

Finally, storytelling is a way of doing justice to a marketing paradigm shift that is in progress as you are engaged in the old-fashioned activity of reading this book. In the past, brands have sent promotional messages to consumers, hoping that consumers would hear those messages and respond by buying the promoted product. In the future, brands will have to hold their own as parts of a growing network of social relations enabled by participatory media. The way people communicate is changing fundamentally. Conversations used to be bipolar: one person talking to another person. But as the amount of social media users explodes, conversations are becoming multipolar.[7] Users share the stories that move them with those they are connected to through social media, they follow what others have to say, and they interact with people they have never met. Consumers like, share, and comment on what matters to them. Injecting their own stories into this expanding ecosystem is the perfect way for brands to stay in touch with consumers today.

Definitions

- Content marketing: A marketing school of utilizing content in order to improve on marketing KPIs. It is often referred to as the art of communicating with your customers without selling.
- Branded content: Editorial content as usually found on the platform where it is published, but clearly branded and often labelled as "sponsored". Branded content can take the shape of a branded social media page or a special story in a magazine.
- Storytelling: A method of explaining a series of events through narrative. By following a story, consumers develop emotional bonds to its characters and elements. Brands can use storytelling as a form of branded content.

- Native advertising: Paid media embedded in the look and feel of the natural publishing environment. For the audience, it is often hard to distinguish native advertisement from editorial content.

How to drive marketing performance using storytelling

Telling stories is what makes us human. Stories shape our lives, and some of the strongest bonds are formed by the stories we tell one another.[8] Storytelling is a natural way of generating attention, sustaining interest, and creating emotional bonds with an audience. In a marketing context, storytelling fosters positive associations between the story told and the brand sold − provided you tell the right stories, and tell them well. Telling the right stories is about content fit, i.e., finding the type of narrative that fits the category you compete in, your brand, and your target group. Telling these stories well is about creative fit, i.e., superior craftsmanship and execution when it comes to the creation of story-driven campaigns. Successful stories typically excel in multiple disciplines in both of these dimensions:

- Content fit: be relevant, be consistent, be differentiated, be credible, and be motivating.
- Creative fit: be original, be simple, be inventive, and be emotional.

Both dimensions are equally important. Content fit helps your campaign register as relevant with your target audience. Appropriate content is in line with your brand identity, and it matches the mental image consumers have formed of your brand. Telling the right story helps you reserve the right to play. To win, you have to get creative in the way you tell your story. Creativity will let a story resonate with its audience and incite people to make a purchase.

According to our research, the right balance of creativity and content fit varies by category. As a general rule, creativity is most effective for products with high emotional involvement, while content fit is paramount to drive sales of commodity-type products that command lower consumer involvement. The best campaigns, however, excel in both dimensions by bringing the brand to life in a way that is as congenial to the spirit of the brand as it is creative in the way the story is told.[9] Says Google's CMO Lorraine Twohill: "If we are going to interrupt you with something that we think is important to you, we have to find a way to tell you about it so that it resonates with you. There has to be a benefit to you. So we tell real-life stories."[10]

Be relevant

"I am always amazed to see just how many things there are that I don't need." The quote is attributed to Socrates, but it expresses a sentiment we are all familiar with. There is too much of everything. Myriads of messages are vying for our attention when we switch on the phone, step into a store, flick through a magazine, or simply walk the street. For a story to register as relevant on our cognitive radar, we have to see the connection between the narrative and our lives. In the context of content marketing, this means that the target audience has to be able to relate to the message. An effective story draws consumers in, provides them with useful information, or even helps them solve some real-life problem they are struggling with. The topics that consumers talk about in social media are a good starting point for the creation of relevant stories, and the best ones incite consumers to participate, i.e., to share the story with others, comment on it, continue telling it, or even create their own spin-off stories.

Apple's award-winning "Shot on iPhone 6" campaign is an example of involving consumers in the storytelling from the beginning. The campaign, created by TWBA's Media Art Lab, features real pictures taken by real people, using the iPhone. The images were reproduced in print ads and posted on thousands of giant billboards in more than

70 cities worldwide. Apple called it "the largest mobile photography gallery in history".[11] Tipp-Ex, the maker of office supplies, was similarly successful with its interactive "hunter and bear birthday party" ad on YouTube. Halfway through the clip, a fiery meteor approaches the scene, and users are presented with a choice ("end the party" or "don't end the party"). The story reached more than 10 million users to date.[12]

Including your audience in the stories that you tell, and inviting it to partake in the telling, are great ways of attracting attention. To sustain the momentum, successful companies direct consumers from paid and earned media to proprietary platforms, such as a brand's user forum. Apple, for example, did not stop at claiming that the iPhone helps users explore and express their creativity. Rather, the company went on to demonstrate how the brand's products enrich consumers' lives. Apple invited users to submit videos shot with their phones and published these clips through the company's iPhone world gallery on TV, in rich-media web ads, and on apple.com.

Be consistent

Our cognitive capacity may be limited, but we respond well to triggers we are already familiar with.[13] Our values and attitudes are shaped by repeated exposure to similar stimuli. So a great way to hold the attention of consumers is to make sure the stories you tell are consistent. As a brand owner, you should find a theme that carries across all stories you tell about your brand. To maximize the effect, consistency should govern not only the stories themselves, but your publishing strategy as well: the styles and formats you use, the media platforms you choose for dissemination, and the timing of individual releases.

John Lewis, the British retailer, is a true master of consistent storytelling. For almost a decade now, the company's Christmas ads have explored recurring themes that include love, friendship, and giving. While the style of execution varies, the emotional key notes are always present. Introduced in 2007, the annual Christmas ad has become a much-anticipated national event in the UK that drives John Lewis' social media followership and sales.[14]

Be differentiated

While you want your stories to be consistent across installments and over time, a good story also needs to be sufficiently different from the stories your competitors are telling. Differentiated storytelling helps you stand out from the noise in your marketplace, and makes it easier for consumers to make the connection between the story and your brand. You don't want to waste your budget on a story that the audience does not associate with your brand, or one that is erroneously attributed to another brand. Nothing is quite as frustrating as spending money to promote your competitor.

Mercedes' 2013 dancing chicken commercial is an impressive example of the impact of differentiated storytelling. When Mercedes first aired the tongue-in-cheek clip to advertise the company's new car body control technology, it generated over 12 million views, and 8 percent of those who saw it shared it with others. When other car manufacturers tried to replicate Mercedes' success by airing similar themed ads, they generated less than a third of the impact. What's more, the copycat competitors drove a lot of additional traffic to the Mercedes original.[15]

Be credible

There is a paradox at the heart of successful storytelling. You want to use stories to build your brand, but you don't want to be caught doing it. In other words, you want it to promote your proposition without appearing promotional. Says Shane Smith, CEO of Vice Media: "Young people have been marketed to since they were newborns. They have developed the most sophisticated bullshit detector, and the only way to circumvent that bullshit detector is to not bullshit them."[16]

To be perceived as credible, start with a genuine message that is true to your brand and honest about the benefits it provides. Then add an authentic messenger with a well-chosen testimonial consumers can relate to, or even an actual consumer who sees eye-to-eye with your target audience. Top it off with an appropriate platform, such as a social media network or a testimonial's personal platform, to get the word out.

Vodafone and Always are among the brands blazing the trail for the integration of real people and everyday situations into marketing communication. In Vodafone's "Firsts" campaign, real-life people are seen fulfilling their lifelong dreams. Vodafone made professional, documentary-style films chronicling these adventures that created a stir in social media.[17] Always' "Like a girl" campaign features real girls talking about their experiences and their feelings. The clips were widely applauded for challenging stereotypes about what it means to be a girl and collectively created close to 100 million views.[18] See the insert below for details.

The girl power story

In 2015, Procter & Gamble's female hygiene brand Always launched "Unstoppable", a campaign that aims at enhancing the confidence of the brand's target group: young girls and women. As part of the campaign, Always uploaded the "#LikeAGirl" video to YouTube. In the clip, real girls speak about what it feels like when others say they are acting "like a girl." They demonstrate what it really means to run, throw, or fight like a girl. The gist is that "like a girl" should not be seen as an insult, but an affirmation of female self-confidence. This video alone attracted about 60 million views.

The campaign was not limited to social media. It was also activated in the offline world. For example, Always hosted the

#LikeAGirl Summit. Additionally, the brand launched a Global Confidence Teaching Curriculum that draws on the latest research on confidence building. This curriculum is intended to reach up to 20 million girls in 65 countries per year. Always also entered into a partnership with TED, the non-profit conference operator, to provide teachers with confidence-related content worth sharing with their students. Zuriel Oduwole, a Nigerian teenager who advocates the empowerment of girls through education, is an ambassador of the campaign. Most recently, Always produced a film in which girls and women tell the stories of what makes them unstoppable. The clip drew 38 million views to date.

According to Always, 50 percent of the brand's teenage and adolescent target audience were exposed to the campaign. Average weekly sales of Always pads were up by 6 percent over the course of the fiscal year after the "Like a girl" clip was launched.

Be motivating

You want your stories to touch and entertain your audience. But that isn't all you want. As a marketer, you also want to influence consumers' attitude and behaviour. You want them to make the connection between the story and the brand, and you want them to buy your products. To fully satisfy the content fit requirement, stories need to drive the performance of your brand in the consumer's decision-making process; see Chapter 3 for details on the different stages consumers go through on the way to purchase. A great story will make consumers like, consider, buy, and recommend your brand.

To connect the story to the brand, look for distinctive assets that make it easy for the audience to figure out who sent the message.

Visual and emotional cues, such as a specific design or a specific set of values, help the audience make that connection, and they also act as potential purchase triggers. Traditional examples of such cues include the shape of the classic Coca-Cola bottle and Apple's white earphones.[19] Make generous use of the assets that you have, or come up with new ways to flag your brand. Only a story that consumers associate with your brand has the potential to drive awareness, positive sentiment, and sales.

Great brands master the challenge of telling compelling stories that are linked to the brand and its products in a subtle way. Examples include Procter & Gamble's "Better for baby" Pampers campaign and Nivea's "Learn to swim" programme, a charitable initiative that features an iconic seahorse mascot decked out in the brand's unique shade of blue.

To effect a change in behaviour, do not hesitate to include explicit calls to action in your stories. Brands are using different types of incentives to encourage their target groups to get active. For example, Dunkin Donuts runs a Halloween photo campaign, asking friends of the brand to dress up as coffee cups and post photos of their costumes on Instagram.[20] Urban transport innovator Uber combines branded storytelling with the distribution of vouchers that encourage users to take a ride.

Be original

Great stories should not only be different from the stories others tell, they also should contain some element or aspect that makes them unique. Perhaps the most notorious example is the space jump Red Bull helped daredevil Felix Baumgartner prepare and execute, something nobody had done before. Records were broken both in terms of the actual jump and in terms of the attention it generated (see insert for details).

Of course, you can only make history every once in a while. Another way of being original is to have your branded stories bounce off breaking news or other current events and affairs. To make this strategy work, you need to be fast. Be the first to tie a branded story to a hot topic, and you will earn the privilege of owning that particular topic. Provided the story also has the appropriate content fit, it will make your brand the talk of the town. This is precisely what Beats by Dre, the headphone brand, accomplished when soccer superstar Bastian Schweinsteiger announced that he would leave Bayern Munich to join Manchester United. Within 24 hours of the press release, Beats launched their "By your side" campaign.[21] Oreo is another fast mover in this area. During the power blackout during the 2013 Super Bowl, the brand responded in real time on Twitter: "Power out? No problem. You can still dunk in the dark."

The adrenaline story

The story Red Bull has built around its brand is so striking that it drives brand attribution and beverage sales without having to refer to the product anymore. Extreme sports and adrenaline junkies are the defining elements of this narrative. The indirect approach has made Red Bull the brand of choice for those who like to think of themselves as adventurous, daring, and competitive. Red Bull aspires not only to create excitement among consumers, but to turn them into fans. Says Red Bull CEO Dietrich Mateschitz: "The most dangerous thing for a branded product is low interest. Brands need to take the phrase 'acting like a publisher' literally."[22]

Red Bull tells its story about extreme sports and adrenaline along several dimensions. The brand sponsors skiing, ski-jumping, and soccer. It also has its own sports teams, such as their branded Formula 1 racing team, a soccer club (SV Red Bull Salzburg), and an ice hockey club (EHC Red Bull Munich). Red Bull also hosts branded events, such as Red Bull Dolomitenmann, Red Bull Vertigo, and Red Bull X-Alps.

The Red Bull story may be rooted in the offline world of arenas, race tracks, and mountain faces, but is fastidiously activated online. The brand supports and exhibits extreme sport content on digital platforms such as Twitter, Facebook, and Instagram. For example, owners of popular sports images on Instagram are rewarded with free trips to popular sports events. Red Bull has also built a notable owned media presence through its Red Bull Media House that manages all of the brand's own media content and social media platforms. On YouTube, more than 3.7 million users have subscribed to the Red Bull channel.

The space jump is Red Bull's most successful storytelling venture to date (Exhibit 4.1). According to Guinness World

Exhibit 4.1   Visual from Red Bull's "Stratos" campaign.
Source: Red Bull

Records, the stunt broke no less than five records. For example, Felix Baumgartner was the first human being to break the sound barrier without any kind of engine power. The campaign drew over 37 million views on YouTube. Global beverage sales increased by 13 percent compared with the year before the jump.[23,24]

Be simple

Consumer attention is in short supply, and it is much contested. Keep your stories simple to cut through the clutter. Your window of opportunity is narrow, so make sure your story can be found quickly and absorbed easily. Shoot for short sentences and plain words. But wording is only one aspect of simple storytelling. You will also want to focus on one message at a time, and use memorable visuals to support it. Colours, symbols, and icons help consumers get that message. Ask yourself a set of simple questions: How does this story bring out our brand promise? How does it tie in with other activities? Which product is the story about? Why should consumers want it?

Nike is a pioneer of simplicity. Their claim, invented by Dan Wieden and introduced in 1988 despite corporate reservations, is straight to the point: "Just do it." The many stories Nike tells about athletes and their accomplishments in advertising all revolve around this spirit: they just do it. The claim is short and simple, and yet it encapsulates the activity, the athleticism, and the motivation Nike stands for as a brand.

Be inventive

Even the best story doesn't share itself. So take every precaution for your story to go viral. Include "like" and "share" buttons for all relevant social media platforms, and make it easy for users to embed your story in their own channels or blogs. If the audience likes, shares, and reposts your story, its reach will multiply at no additional cost to you. What's more, a story recommended by a friend, or by someone you follow, is more likely to register as relevant and credible on your radar than a story some company wants you to read or see. Organic sharing drives relevant reach and brings down cost per view. For example, the Melbourne Metro Trains campaign "Dumb ways to die" was viewed more than 100 million times on YouTube, simply by way of social media distribution.

And if it works once, it might work again. Why stop telling an exciting story that consumers want to see and hear more of? Adopt a publisher's mindset and take inspiration from the likes of Ian Fleming, Stan Lee, George Lucas, and J. K. Rowling. Serial production will help you build a fan base that eagerly awaits the next installment of branded content. Apple pulled it off with their now legendary "Get a Mac" campaign. Featuring actors John Hodgeman as the boring PC and Justin Long as the hip Mac, the series comprises more than 60 episodes. The campaign ran for more than three years and received a Grand Effie award in 2007. AdWeek declared it the "best advertising campaign of the decade" in 2010.

Be emotional

Would you care for another bland commercial? Probably not. Most people don't. We are all at turns overwhelmed and annoyed by generic advertising. The challenge for branded stories is to get past the brain's screening mechanisms and trigger a positive reaction. You want your audience to want to see your story again. But how do you do that? By appealing to emotion. Emotional campaigns are often particularly successful, both in terms of likeability and in terms of purchase generation. Behavioural science has demonstrated that emotions are important drivers of human decision making and behaviour. When consumers are confronted with a purchase decision, they evaluate each option based on what they have felt in previous, related experiences.[25] Says John Kearon, CEO of Brain Juicer, a two-time winner of Esomar's best methodology award: "We are basically emotional creatures. We think much less than we think we think. And what marketing and advertising overdoes is trying to persuade people to buy, whereas actually they should try and seduce people to buy."[26]

The aforementioned John Lewis Christmas campaign is a fine example not only of consistency, but also of emotional storytelling. Launched in 2007, the series has since broken many records. In 2013, John Lewis ran with "The bear and the hare", a very emotional episode and arguably the most successful one to date. The clip was watched over 15 million times on YouTube and eventually became the most shared video in the world.[27] It generated GBP 142 million in incremental sales and had one of the highest ROIs ever observed by the jurors of the Creative Effectiveness Lions, GBP 7.21 for every GBP 1 spent on advertising.[28]

The motherhood story

What do detergents, diapers, cough drops, and shampoo have in common? Tough call. For a long time, Procter & Gamble didn't have an answer. Consequently, the company chose not to activate its corporate brand. Advertising was focused on the brands and products in the company's extensive portfolio, from cleaning supplies to personal care.

On the occasion of the 2012 Olympics, P&G started telling an emotional story about its corporate brand. The topic they chose was how Procter & Gamble is in the business of making the lives of mothers easier ("proud sponsor of moms"), a theme that stretches from household products to health and beauty care. The story was told across multiple channels. On TV, P&G

ran emotional commercials. The "Best job" TV commercial, for example, was about thanking moms for the daily sacrifices they make for their families. Another one, "Kids", focused on the fact that even grown-up athletes will always be kids in the eyes of their moms. Additionally, P&G created long-form content, including a series of short films called "Raising an Olympian", featuring portraits of women who had actually done it. With the help of various apps, P&G enabled users to thank their own moms with videos, photos, and texts. And as part of NBC's coverage of the games, real footage of proud mothers of successful athletes appeared in branded clips that were shown instead of traditional TV commercials during commercial breaks. P&G also took care of athletes' mothers by defraying the cost of their travel to the games, providing them with homes away from home, meals, laundry service, and beauty treatments.

Procter & Gamble considers the campaign a milestone on its way to a more caring brand image. The TV advertising generated a brand recall of 40 percent, well ahead of other high-profile Olympics sponsors. The "Best job" clip was among the most-shared ads in 2012. This wasn't just a TV advertising story. The company also used it to create cross-brand activation in stores and drive impact at retail. In the US, the campaign generated USD 200 million in incremental sales, twice the uplift P&G had anticipated.[29]

By the way, this chapter runs to about 5,000 words. It would have taken Bob Andrews, the veteran of soap opera screenwriting, roughly four hours, three dozen cigarettes, and a gallon of coffee to complete. But they don't make hacks quite as productive, and as frugal, as Bob Andrews anymore. Chances are that today's master content marketers will pester you with questions about your brand, while insisting on celery sticks and kale smoothies for sustenance.

So stock up on organic goodies, brace yourself for some serious brainstorming, and find yourself a storyteller.

Key takeaways

- Be relevant. Find out what consumers care about and give them opportunities to become part of the stories you tell about your brand.
- Be consistent. Pick a theme that carries across different stories to hold the attention of your target group over an extended period of time.
- Be differentiated. Go where no other brand has gone before. Nobody likes a copycat, and generic stories run a high risk of being attributed to the wrong brand.
- Be credible. Look for topics, testimonials, and platforms that will strike users as believable extensions of your brand into the world they live in.
- Be motivating. Link the stories you tell to your brand and its products. Include explicit calls to action for consumers.
- Be original. Come up with unique stories that capture the spirit of the moment. Move fast to claim breaking news and hot topics for your brand.
- Be simple. Use plain language and visual cues to make it easy for consumers to find, understand, and remember your stories.
- Be inventive. Take every precaution for your stories to go viral. And once they do, give people more of what they like by investing in serial production.
- Be emotional. Appeal to consumers' feelings to drive likeability and trigger purchase decisions.

NOTES

1. James Thurber, "Soapland I – O Pioneers!," *The New Yorker*, 15 May 1948, pp. 34–47; http://www.chicagonow.com/interesting-chicago/2014/03/robert-hardy-andrews/;https://www.otrcat.com/p/ma-perkins.

2. *Soap Opera: The Inside Story of Procter & Gamble*, by Alecia Swasy, Crown, 2012.
3. NetCraft and Internet Live Stats.
4. Nielsen, HIS.
5. According to Nielsen, TV usage has declined by almost a third over the course of the last five years.
6. For example, Coca-Cola went from one brand, and one product, in 1886 to a portfolio of hundreds of brands and thousands of products today (http://www.coca-colacompany.com/brands/all/).
7. According to SNL Kagan, the number of Facebook users alone jumped from 680 million to 1.4 billion in just over four years.
8. *The Storytelling Animal: How Stories Make us Human*, by Jonathan Gottschall, Mariner Books, New York, 2013.
9. In a pioneering study, McKinsey & Company's Marketing and Sales Practice, in collaboration with the Art Directors Club for Germany (ADC) and the Berlin School of Creative Leadership, has defined quantifiable metrics for both creativity and content fit to determine their relative impact on advertising effectiveness; see Jesko Perrey, Nicola Wagener, and Carsten Wallmann, "Kreativität oder Content Fit – Was wirkt besser in der Werbung?" *Akzente*, 2007, Number 3, pp. 16–21.
10. http://www.mckinsey.com/insights/marketing_sales/how_google_breaks_through.
11. http://techcrunch.com/2015/06/01/apples-shot-on-iphone-6-campaign-expand-with-new-user-films/; http://www.adweek.com/news/advertising-branding/apple-tbwa-take-outdoor-grand-prix-billboards-featuring-users-iphone-6-photos-165516.
12. https://www.youtube.com/watch?v=eQtai7HMbuQ.
13. *Integrative Umweltbewertung*, by Werner Theobald, Springer, Berlin/Heidelberg, 1998, pp. 46–49.
14. http://www.marketingmagazine.co.uk/article/1320008/john-lewis-christmas-ads-2007-2014-humble-roots-national-event.
15. http://www.ameawards.com/winners/2015/pieces-mobile.php?iid=481970&pid=2.
16. http://www.theguardian.com/media/2014/mar/02/vice-media-shane-smith-north-korea.
17. https://www.vidyard.com/blog/vodafone-soars-to-storytelling-glory-by-capturing-video-firsts/.
18. http://www.adweek.com/news/advertising-branding/hugely-popular-girl-campaign-always-will-return-sunday-super-bowl-ad-162619.
19. *How Brands Grow*, by Bryan Sharpe, Oxford University Press, Oxford, 2010.
20. http://www.business2community.com/social-media/the-effect-of-instagram-contests-analyzing-dunkin-donuts-dressedd-0328219#vmZUOgbEJr2zqqTP.97.

21. http://www.horizont.net/marketing/nachrichten/Bastian-Schweinsteigers-Abschied-aus-Muenchen-Beats-by-Dre-zeigt-wie-emotionales-Storytelling-geht-135328.
22. http://www.bloomberg.com/bw/magazine/content/11_22/b4230064852768.htm; https://medium.com/art-marketing/your-brand-s-silver-bullet-729544e9de79.
23. http://adage.com/article/special-report-marketer-alist-2013/red-bull-stratos-space-jump-helped-sell-a-lot-product/243751/.
24. https://www.brandwatch.com/2014/11/3-brands-get-storytelling-right-can/.
25. *Descartes' Error: Emotion, Reason, and the Human Brain*, by Anthony Damasio, Penguin Books, 2005. Found via https://www.psychologytoday.com/blog/inside-the-consumer-mind/201302/how-emotions-influence-what-we-buy.
26. https://www.youtube.com/watch?v=hmN_ZhzAlmY.
27. www.warc.com. "John Lewis: The bear and the hare", Cannes Creative Lions, Gold – Creative effectiveness Lions – 2015.
28. http://www.marketingmagazine.co.uk/article/1320008/john-lewis-christmas-ads-2007-2014-humble-roots-national-event; http://www.campaignlive.co.uk/article/1227555/bear-hare-ad-sends-alarm-clock-sales-soaring-john-lewis.
29. www.warc.com. Procter & Gamble: London 2012 Olympic Games – Thank you Mom. ARF Ogilvy Awards, Grand Ogilvy and Gold – Sports, Entertainment and Media – 2013.

5 – ONE CURRENCY

Compare apples to apples as you make trade-offs between instruments

Why does one currency matter?

Marketing mix optimization can feel a lot like travelling in medieval Europe, with its dozens of currencies and unpredictable conversion rates. There are several dozen marketing instruments already – from TV to Twitter – and new ones keep popping up all the time. Many of these instruments come with their own metrics and KPIs (Exhibit 5.1). While media agencies often rely on established metrics like GRPs (gross rating points[1]) or CPM (cost per mille[2]) for classical advertising, new media bring their own currencies, such as the number of likes and followers in social networks. To make things worse, a lot of specialized vendors work with proprietary performance indicators. And for some instruments – such as out-of-home advertising – there are no well-established metrics at all, or advertisers just don't track them. As a marketer, you have no easy way of comparing all the different indicators. How do you convert prime-time TV ratings into Facebook followers? What is more valuable, a thousand clicks on a thumb-sized online banner, or a hundred visitors exposed to larger-than-life banners for three hours at a sponsored sporting event?

All this is tricky enough for one brand competing in a single category and sold in one country. But who has the luxury of such focus? Most senior marketers today are juggling an international portfolio of

Instrument	Metrics (examples, not exhaustive)
Online • Own website	• Unique visitors, time spent, bounce rate
• Facebook link	• Likes, shares, page views, sentiment
• Display advertising	• Impressions, reach, click-through rate, conversion
• Online video ads	• Views, click-through rate, completion rate
• SEA	• Cost per click, cost per lead, ranking
• Facebook brand page	• Fans, likes, shares, comments, sentiment
• Apps	• Downloads, app store ranking, session time
Direct • SMS	• Send-outs, opening rate, conversion
• Outbound calls	• Conversion, leads generated, data gathered
• Mailing	• Response rate, cost per lead
• E-mail	• Send-outs, opening rate, click rate, conversion
POS • POS materials	• Number distributed, sales uplift
• Leaflet	• Number distributed, response quote, sales uplift
PR/ event • PR	• Media equivalent, press clippings, no. of readers, sentiment
• Event/sponsoring	• Spectators, media coverage, online views
Media • Print magazine	• Reach, cost per thousand
• Radio ads	• Reach (number of listeners), share of voice
• TV	• GRP, cost per thousand, share of voice
• Cinema	• Reach, cost per thousand, share of voice
• Outdoor poster	• Reach, cost per thousand, share of voice

Exhibit 5.1   Marketing instruments and common metrics.
Source: McKinsey

brands and products, all with different target groups and conflicting objectives. For example, a newly launched product line or sub-brand calls for mass media to generate attention and attract first-time buyers. Sustaining a product or tariff that approaches the end of its life cycle, however, is typically more about keeping existing customers amused and engaged through direct channels. In many cases, different budget owners and decision makers will be involved at different levels of the organization. And no two countries are the same, neither in terms of the instruments that are available nor in terms of regulation. For a given brand or product, an instrument that is a central part of the marketing mix in one country may not be available at all in another. There are severe restrictions, for example, when it comes to advertising tobacco through above-the-line media in many countries. The same is true for impact measurement. While certain metrics or analytical approaches are commonplace in one territory, they are difficult to establish elsewhere in the world.

Put yourself in the shoes of a mobile operator. How on earth do you figure out whether sending out a bunch of virtual vouchers for free data to current subscribers in Turkey beats a mass media launch campaign for the next-generation handset in Brazil? While it may be possible to optimize individual instruments (see Chapter 7), most marketers are at a loss when it comes to allotting funds across media, business units, brands, products, and countries. As a result, we see one of two things happening. Some CMOs play it safe and simply stick to current practices: "What did we do last year? 60 percent classical, 20 percent direct, 10 percent sponsorship, and 10 percent online? Sounds good to me. Let's keep doing that." Others have effectively given up and handed their budgets to the agencies: "These guys are the experts, and we pay them good money to screen the media landscape for us. Let's go with their recommendation." Chances are that neither of these approaches will maximize the return on your marketing investment. We believe that you should be in charge of your budget, supported by the facts and the means to judge and improve marketing mix decisions.

How to drive marketing performance with one currency

To overcome the near-Babylonian confusion of media and metrics, we have developed the Reach-Cost-Quality (RCQ) approach (Exhibit 5.2). The score this approach yields is a common currency that lets you compare marketing instruments irrespective of their history, mode of action, or technological platform. As a universal metric, RCQ helps you make like-for-like comparisons between different instruments and optimize your marketing mix accordingly. Depending on your business objectives and marketing strategy (see Chapter 1), you can either use RCQ to increase actual reach and

Exhibit 5.2 Reach-Cost-Quality.
Source: McKinsey

contact quality without changing your total budget (i.e., to increase effectiveness), or to reduce costs without compromising advertising impact (i.e., to increase efficiency). The approach was first deployed about ten years ago and has since successfully been adopted by hundreds of companies.[3]

To be able to apply RCQ consistently and take advantage of holistic optimization, you need to quantify each of its components for all marketing instruments.

- R = reach, i.e., the actual number of people reached in the relevant target group.
- C = cost, i.e., the full cost associated with a particular instrument.
- Q = quality, i.e., the impact an instrument has on the consumer it reaches.

Any consumer touch point qualifies as an instrument, from newspaper advertising and TV commercials to POS materials and YouTube videos related to your brand. In this chapter, we look at the success factors that will let you reap the full benefit of RCQ for your company. But don't think that RCQ will rid you of your duties as a decision maker. On the contrary. The common currency is intended as a resource that helps you reclaim control over your budget from self-appointed gurus and their black boxes. It provides you with the fact base, the transparency, and the common language you need to make informed decisions and discuss them with your fellow executives and external partners.

Although RCQ scoring is a big improvement over rules of thumb, it has certain built-in limitations that are rooted in its relative simplicity. For example, it assesses each marketing instrument separately. As a result, RCQ does not account for interaction effects between instruments, e.g., between advertising and promotions, or between TV and digital. Only advanced analytical approaches – such as multivariate regression or attribution modelling – can do that.[4] Advanced analytics can also help improve the accuracy of individual RCQ components, such as the actual reach in your target group and the effectiveness (the "quality") of this reach. See the next chapter for details on advanced analytics.

Be specific about your target group

Official documents and corporate memos are often labelled "to whom it may concern." The RCQ approach requires you to be a little more specific about your target group. In order to quantify the actual "R" component for each marketing instrument, you want to be as precise as possible about your target group. This is because the reach of any one instrument is very different for different target groups, and the total reach of an instrument can be highly misleading. For example, Facebook reported 1.5 billion active users in 2015.[5] But while Facebook may be well suited to reach a middle-aged audience in Western Europe and North America, its reach among teenagers is fading rapidly.[6] And while advertising on daytime TV may get you cheap exposure to millions of viewers, are these really the people that matter to you? To get a more realistic reach figure for a particular marketing instrument, subtract those who are not in your target group for a given product or campaign.

The result of this process is often referred to as "relevant reach." It gives due credit to those media – be they classical, digital, or local – that are best suited to reach your audience, and depreciate those instruments that produce a lot of scatter losses. For example, not all visitors of a car show will be in the target group for all exhibitors. From the perspective of a luxury brand, only a fraction of those who marvel at cars carrying six-figure sticker prices qualify as potential buyers. The devil is in the detail though. It's simple enough for direct media, such as addressed mail. You just send it to people in your target group – period. The same applies to outbound e-mails and calls. By default, total reach gets very close to relevant reach for direct media. But broadcast media – such as TV or radio – are more challenging. At face value, one TV contact looks a lot cheaper than one contact generated through an addressed mailing. This is because TV gives you a lot of contacts that are not relevant. The audience most media agencies work with often includes everyone in a certain age bracket, e.g., 14 to 49. You need to take out all those who don't fit the bill of your target group.

- Demographic: Start by subtracting everyone who is outside the age range of your target group, i.e., too young or too old. And if you are advertising female hygiene products, subtract all men. You get the idea.
- Sociographic: Subtract everyone who doesn't fit the income bracket you are targeting. And as a retailer, be sure to exclude those who live outside the catchment area of one of your stores.
- Psychographic: Subtract all those who don't share the attitudes and values your brand or product appeals to. If you represent a luxury brand, subtract the cheapskates. Note that psychographic data will not always be available.

When you are done, it will become apparent that mass media can be a lot more costly than they appear at first sight. You may be surprised by how little remains of the supposedly high reach of classic instruments, or by how effectively some low-profile niche media reach specific target groups.

Account for missed opportunities to see

Have you ever snuck away from the TV during a commercial break to go to the bathroom, feed the cat, or get a snack for yourself? Yes? Everyone does. But there is a bigger issue at stake here, and it affects the way a marketing instrument scores in RCQ analysis. Even once you have narrowed down total reach to relevant reach for a given instrument, that figure is still somewhat theoretical. It represents opportunities to see (OTS[7]) an advertisement, rather than actual exposure or recall.

For example, it is hard to escape a 60-second trailer that is screened before the main feature at a cinema, especially since many movie-goers consider trailers a part of the cinematic experience. The likelihood that a ticketholder will later recall the trailer can be as high as 80 percent, counting out a few latecomers and those whose eyes are glued to their phones until the movie starts. But what about a billboard by the side of the road? How many times do you drive past that before you even notice it? Most people will need multiple opportunities to see a billboard before they actually notice it, let alone recall what it says. The tune-out effect is typically even higher for online media. Many online ads are displayed outside the area of the screen that is visible to a given user, when the user is not paying attention to the screen, or is away from the computer, tablet, or phone altogether. As a result, multiple ad impressions are required before someone actually gets to see and absorb an online ad.

To get from theoretical reach to actual reach and advertising recall, you need to account for those who should have been reached in theory, but missed their opportunity to see your ad. Ask your media agency to estimate the number of opportunities to see for each person reached (n), as well as the likelihood to recall an ad per opportunity to see (b). Based on this information, you can calculate effective recall, using the formula $1-(1-b)^n$. To increase recall in your target group, it is often more effective to switch to an instrument with a higher likelihood to recall per OTS, rather than to increase the number of opportunities to see for a given instrument.

Take a full cost perspective

How much does it cost you to drive to work? Easy. Let's say it's 10 miles from your house to the office. Gas mileage for your SUV is 20 miles per gallon. So you need half a gallon to make the one-way trip. A gallon of regular costs 2 dollars, so your cost for the one-way commute is 1 dollar. That's so much cheaper than public transport! No reason to cram yourself into a smelly subway car. What a relief. But hold on. Are you being honest with yourself? What about the cost of buying or leasing the SUV? What about maintenance, insurance, and depreciation?

The "C" in RCQ is defined as the full cost that is caused by an instrument, often referred to as the "total cost of ownership" for a given consumer touch point. Much like gas consumption for a car, media buying cost is just the most obvious position for a marketing vehicle. While it is often also the largest bucket for classical media, some instruments come with substantial additional cost. For example, the cost of TV advertising includes creative agency fees and production cost. Other instruments may not require you to buy advertising space at all, but can come with their own types of hidden cost. Consider owned digital media, like a Facebook profile or the company home page. Because you don't pay activation fees for these instruments, you might be tempted to think that they give you free reach. But what about that hotshot social media manager on your payroll? What about the research your agency conducts to find out which topics you should tweet about? What about the software licence fee for the content management system that sits at the back end of your home page?

To avoid distortion, you need to include all costs that can be linked to a given instrument – be they internal or external, variable or

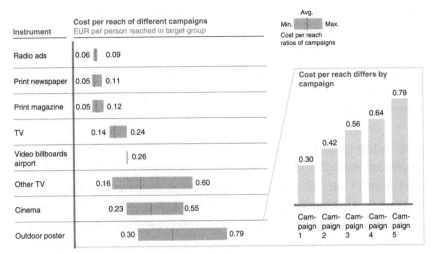

Exhibit 5.3 Cost per reach across different instruments (example).
Source: McKinsey

fixed-step. Don't overdo it though. If someone on your team develops content that is activated both online and offline, their salary should not be attributed to any one instrument, or only proportionally so. For example, the work of your chief storyteller (see last chapter) might be featured in a YouTube clip, an old-school advertorial in a magazine, and in a direct mail campaign.

Using qualified reach and total cost, you can already rank different instruments in your mix according to their efficiency in reaching your target group (Exhibit 5.3). Please note that this is just an example, and that the numbers will be different in another country, industry, or context.

Evaluate contact quality based on your business objectives

Chances are that "total cost per qualified reach" is already a lot more insightful as a metric than anything your media agency will come up with. To make the analysis even more powerful, and create a more differentiated fact base for robust mix decisions, we encourage you to include "quality" as well. It will bring out the specific strengths and weaknesses of different marketing instruments even more clearly. In the context of RCQ, contact quality – or "quality of touch" – is defined as the effectiveness of an instrument in reaching your marketing and business objectives.

Despite the pitfalls discussed above, calculating reach and cost is a relatively straightforward exercise. Quantifying contact quality is a little harder. There are different approaches to doing this with varying degrees of sophistication. Some are more data intensive, others are more intuitive. Most companies differentiate between short-term and long-term objectives and classify marketing vehicles accordingly.

- Short-term objectives: drive revenues, volume, or customer acquisition.
- Long-term objectives: build brand equity and customer retention.

While direct mail is well suited to drive sales, a Facebook profile is more relevant with respect to the long-term performance of your brand. Depending on the content of a given commercial, TV advertising may serve both short-term and long-term objectives. As you evaluate instrument effectiveness, make sure to review any past performance data you may have. Don't hesitate to have external providers – such as your media planner or online marketing agency – assemble and review this type of data for you. Opening rates for direct mail, conversion rates for online ads linked to your e-commerce store, or the average amount of positive buzz generated by viral videos will help you gauge the fitness of these instruments to support the objectives of your company. While some instruments are particularly well suited to convey information (cognitive quality), others are better at evoking emotion (affective quality) or triggering action (behavioural quality). The car show that we mentioned above is a good example of a touch point with high affective quality. While the reach of such events is certainly limited, the opportunity to experience the goods in real life makes shows and fairs much more powerful as touch points than print ads, television commercials, or glossy brochures.[8]

Another option is to evaluate instruments according to their effectiveness in influencing consumers at different stages of their decision-making process. For example, classical media are well suited to generate initial attention and awareness. In-store promotions, POS materials, and online vouchers typically achieve high-quality scores when it comes to direct impact on the purchase decision. In contrast, brand-related events, reward programmes, or online communities are often better suited to sustain customer loyalty. Proven approaches to modelling the decision-making process include the brand purchase funnel (see Chapter 3) and the consumer decision journey (see Chapter 6).

For an even more differentiated view on instrument effectiveness, you may want to assess the instruments with regard to multiple objectives – such as brand building versus sales push – and display the results in a matrix (Exhibit 5.4). In this example, cinema advertising and a Facebook page come out as superior brand strength drivers. In contrast, direct marketing instruments – such as outbound calls and e-mails – receive top scores for their sales impact. Please note that this example is purely illustrative, and that the results of this type of analysis will vary with country, industry, and other factors.

Balance analysis with common sense

So now you have rock-solid RCQ scores for all instruments, right? Why not pour your entire budget into the top five and kick back while those dollars work for you? Bad idea. If you follow the numbers blindly, you run a high risk of shipwrecking your marketing plan in some spectacular way. We've seen it happen. In one case, the marketing analytics team at a retail company spent weeks wrangling advanced analytics to optimize online marketing

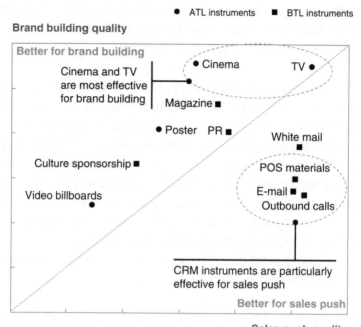

Exhibit 5.4 Contact quality matrix (example).
Source: McKinsey

activities, chiefly because this was the part of the mix for which they had the most detailed performance data. When they were done comparing the impact of pop-up video ads and opt-in newsfeeds, the team realized that online marketing as a whole only accounted for about 5 percent of the retailer's total marketing budget. They had not looked at local leaflets at all – the biggest budget position by far – and a much more important marketing ROI lever than online marketing. But by then, it was time to submit the budget for board approval. They had no choice but to copy over the marketing plan from the year before.

In another case, a maker of consumer goods calculated the ROI for various marketing instruments. Some of these came out negative, and the company duly pulled the plug on those instruments.

The trouble was that they had only accounted for the short-term sales effect in their contact quality assessment. As a result, most of the instruments that primarily supported long-term brand equity and loyalty – such as special events and aftersales support – looked bad: high costs, but little to no immediate sales effect. What the company didn't factor in was that a strong brand is the prerequisite of future sales. Before long, the company saw their net promoter scores, repurchase rates, and other loyalty indicators dwindling. Disappointed customers spread the word about their unsatisfactory post-purchase experience, and eventually sales started to drop.

To avoid such mishaps, we encourage you to balance the facts and figures produced by an RCQ analysis with the judgement and the experience of your team. If in doubt, make an informed estimate to get the mix roughly right, rather than precisely wrong. Why not feed experience into the RCQ score itself? One way of doing this is to gather the experts for a workshop and have them assess the most important instruments in your mix in terms of how well they are suited to support your business objectives. To get a balanced perspective, include your fellow marketers, sales professionals, and the most experienced planners from your media agency. You won't have detailed effectiveness data for all instruments anyway, and even supposedly hard figures like actual reach require some estimates, such as the number of "opportunities to see" a person needs before they notice an ad.

In fact, expert workshops come with several side benefits that make them well worth your while – even if they fail to answer all your questions. A face-to-face discussion, for example, will help you uncover and challenge hidden assumptions or die-hard marketing myths. Keep in mind that it can be hard for seasoned brand or product managers to sit and listen while others are judging their campaigns or the mix of instruments they use. So better let people know that a low score for a particular instrument does not equal a reprimand for whoever is in charge of it, or was in charge in the past. An open mind is a key success factor for such workshops. This is especially important if it is the first time a company is developing a joint perspective across instruments. Make sure everybody has their say, and that participants' concerns are not dismissed without discussion. You will be surprised to find how even former antagonists can work their way towards a shared view of what's best for the company. If you play your cards right, participants will walk away as advocates of systematic marketing mix optimization, and help you defend any changes you may need to make against objections from those who feel you are invading their turf.[9]

Create an integrated performance metric

Total reach adjusted to account for contacts outside your target group and missed opportunities to see? Check. Costs calculated to include the total cost of ownership of each instrument? Check. Contact quality evaluated in light of your business objectives and pressure-tested in expert workshops? Check. You are now ready to derive an integrated performance score: the qualified reach per cost (Exhibit 5.5). This score does not replace a media plan, but it is

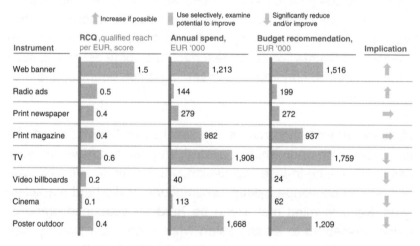

Exhibit 5.5   The qualified reach per cost (example).
Source: McKinsey

a much more solid base for mix decisions than any rule of thumb. It does justice to the real reach, the total cost, and the contact quality of each instrument. As a common currency, it helps you pinpoint past misallocations and identify opportunities to shift parts of the budget to instruments with a higher qualified reach per cost. In combination with minimum and maximum spending thresholds for each instrument, which advanced analysis as described in Chapter 6 will help determine, RCQ serves as the basis for a fact-based mix recommendation. RCQ scores enable you to challenge the recommendations of your media agency – or past practices and habitual allocation patterns – with quantified facts. Like a traveller in the United States or present-day Europe, you can stop worrying about conversion rates and finally start thinking about the best way to spend your money.

Application example: Consumer electronics giant

A manufacturer of consumer electronics had long focused on supplying no-name components to other companies. But as margins decreased, the company started selling to consumers and building its own brand. After about a decade, global marketing spending had reached the threshold of USD 1 billion annually. The high cost position came to the attention of the supervisory board, and a systematic review was initiated.

It turned out that the company used a broad mix of marketing instruments: print advertising, TV commercials, digital media, cofinanced dealer marketing, direct marketing, events, and extensive sports sponsoring. Responsibility for the various budget positions and instruments was scattered all over the organization – from product marketing (for launch campaigns) and sales (for dealer support) to corporate communications (for events, sponsorships, and special projects). As a result, there was no consistent data on the relative impact of different marketing instruments.

In response, the supervisory board charged the CMO with the development of a unified, yet pragmatic, approach to assess and optimize the company's marketing mix. Advanced econometric modelling was not an option. The company's historic data was simply too patchy. What's more, most of the company's products were high-ticket-price items purchased only infrequently. This made it impossible for the CMO's team to derive valid correlations between marketing spending and sales. So the CMO opted for RCQ as the common currency to compare and rank instruments according to their qualified reach. A deep dive was conducted to review sponsorships, a particularly prominent budget position. Some sponsorships were earmarked for increased activation through PR, while others were shortlisted for discontinuation. To support its global growth ambitions, the company did not reduce its marketing budget, but managed to achieve an increase in qualified reach of about 20 percent.

Key takeaways

- Be specific about your target group. Disregard everyone outside your target group to get from total reach to relevant reach for each instrument.
- Account for missed opportunities to see. Most marketing instruments require repeated exposure before an ad actually registers with the user.
- Take a full cost perspective. Capture the total cost of ownership of each marketing instrument, including salaries and agency fees as relevant.

- Evaluate contact quality based on your business objectives. Assess each instrument, e.g., in terms of its fitness for brand building versus sales push.
- Balance analysis with common sense. Conduct expert workshops to pressure-test your instrument evaluation and create alignment among your executive peers.
- Create an integrated performance metric. Rely on the real reach, total cost, and contact quality to compare instruments and optimize your mix.

NOTES

1. http://www.nielsenmedia.com/glossary/terms/G/gross_rating_point.htm.
2. http://www.nielsenmedia.com/glossary/terms/C/#Cost Per Thousand (CPM).
3. http://www.marke41.de/sites/default/files/media/autoren-pdf/die_rcq -formel.pdf.
4. For a detailed discussion of interaction effects, see Prasad Naik, Kalyan Raman, and Russel S. Winer, "Planning marketing mix strategies in the presence of interaction effects," *Marketing Science*, 2005, Volume 24, Number 1, pp. 25–34.
5. http://www.statista.com/statistics/264810/number-of-monthly-active-face book-users-worldwide/.
6. http://www.techtimes.com/articles/30603/20150203/faceook-losing-teen-audience-now-its-just-old-people-socializing.htm.
7. http://www.marketingresearch.org/issues-policies/glossary/opportunities-see-ots.
8. Compare the discussion of marketing ROI in Chapter 4.2 of *Power Brands*, by Jesko Perrey, Dennis Spillecke, and Tjark Freundt, Third Edition, Wiley, 2015.
9. There are also practical limitations to the use of certain touch points. For example, TV advertising only makes sense if funds are sufficient to reach a share of voice that will make sure your campaign is even noticed by consumers. At the same time, incremental returns will decrease beyond a certain investment level. To optimize the entire media mix, combine RCQ scores with thresholds of efficient spend for the different touch points. This avoids overspending on vehicles that – while they might look very attractive because of the low cost per actual reach – will nonetheless lose efficiency beyond a certain saturation point. Similarly, spend thresholds help ensure

that you invest above the minimal level necessary for your communication to be heard despite the competitive noise at a specific touch point. Compare the more detailed discussion of RCQ in Chapter 10 of *Retail Marketing and Branding*, by Jesko Perrey and Dennis Spillecke, Second Edition, John Wiley & Sons, 2013.

6 – SCIENCE

Apply advanced analytics to drive fact-based mix optimization

Why do advanced analytical approaches matter?

What is the perfect mix of marketing instruments and media? We have bad news, and we have good news. The bad news is that the *perfect* mix is a myth. It doesn't exist. The good news is that you are in a better position than any previous generation of CMOs to determine the *right* mix for a given set of strategic parameters and business objectives thanks to a growing treasure trove of marketing performance data. Analytics is the key that unlocks that treasure. We encourage you to upgrade your analytical arsenal to turn data into insight – and insight into action – quickly, flexibly, and on a granular level.

Let's look at some facts. Users perform more than 3.5 billion Google searches per day.[1] A single user will create up to 25 megabytes of data over the course of a single hour of browsing.[2] More than ten digital touch points[3] are involved in a typical online purchase decision journey.[4] Digital marketing already accounts for one-fifth of all marketing spending, and even traditional media afford increasing opportunities for tracking and targeting. For example, the number of users who stream TV over IP connections is growing at a rate of about 30 percent annually.[5] Also, 84 percent of smartphone and tablet owners now use their mobile devices as a second screen while watching TV, and 27 percent look up product information online after watching an ad on TV. These developments make it easier for advertisers to assess the impact of their investments. Across the board, the number and the granularity of observations available for analysis and optimization is increasing continuously. The beauty of it is that you are no longer restricted to hands-off data gathering and processing. Behavioural analysis allows you to integrate big data with your business model and sharpen your value proposition on the fly. Examples include Amazon's fabled recommendation engine and the demand-driven approach to content development perfected by Netflix, the online TV streaming operator.[6]

But it's not just that the amount and complexity of data exceeds the capacity of manual analysis. It's also a question of speed. Until recently, campaign planning and media buying was done months in advance. Today, marketers make adjustments to their campaigns while they run. The bulk of digital media is already traded in real time,[7] usually with the help of automated algorithms – machines dealing with machines. See Chapter 10 for a dedicated discussion of speed as a success factor of high-performing marketing organizations.

Marketing analytics used to be manual, linear, and ex post. In the future, you will have to adopt advanced, automated, live analytics. If you do, you will be making more targeted, more effective, and more efficient investments. If you stick with the old ways, you will be left behind – no matter how big a pile of data you sit on.

How to drive marketing performance with advanced analytics

Ready to graduate from art and craft to science? Great. But hold on. We don't suggest you abandon the art of creative messaging, or the craft of sober management. All we are saying is that it's high time that we infused marketing with an extra shot of science. There are many different approaches to fact-based marketing mix optimization.

In the previous chapter, we discussed Reach-Cost-Quality (RCQ) analysis, a great way for marketers to establish a common currency and a common language to compare instruments[8] on a like-for-like basis. An RCQ score is as good and as meaningful as the data it is based on, and advanced analytics can actually help you quantify – rather than estimate – both the actual reach in your target group and the effectiveness (the "quality") of this reach. Don't aim for perfection though. No single model will ever capture the full complexity of the real world anyway, and we have seen many overly complex models gather dust on the shelf.

In this chapter, we will look at a set of well-established techniques that connect investment to impact. These techniques will help you disaggregate, quantify, and increase the return on marketing investment for individual instruments. As a school of thought, advanced marketing ROI analytics acknowledges the fact that marketing success is influenced by many factors in parallel, and it helps you single out the contribution of each instrument, starting with those that are most relevant to drive your business.

Pick an analytics approach that fits your business situation

Start by taking stock of your industry and the situation of your business. How much data do you have? How far does it go back, and how granular is it in terms of time periods and instruments? Do you collect and store this data yourself, or does someone else further down the value chain own the customer relationship? Is your business model driven by strategic long shots and brand strength, or by tactical communication and millions of small-ticket transactions? What is your primary marketing objective – attention, consideration, or sales stimulation? Refer to the insert below for guidance on how to pick the analytical approach that best fits your needs.

- **Marketing and media mix modelling**: Often referred to as econometric marketing mix modelling, or MMM for short, this technique uses detailed historical data and time series regression analysis to quantify the impact of marketing activities on sales or other dependent variables, such as customer acquisition or lead generation. MMM allows you to adjust for external factors – such as weather or seasonality – to make sure the marketing function is only credited with what it really contributes to business success.

- **Digital attribution:**[9] User-level journey analytics and attribution modelling (often referred to as digital attribution, or DA for short) is a technique that determines the influence of a single touch point on marketing success. This could be, for example, a rich media ad that a user is exposed to prior to the completion of an online transaction. Over the course of a purchase decision journey, a consumer makes contact with a brand at multiple touch points. By analysing many such journeys, DA allows you to do justice to all touch points on the journey and pinpoint the most relevant ones.
- **Consumer survey:** There are various approaches. We often use consumer decision journey research, or CDJ for short. This technique uses questionnaires to take a snapshot of touch point importance as stated by respondents and determine the impact of marketing investments at specific stages of a consumer's decision journey. The emerging fact base helps you focus your investments on the instruments that have the biggest impact on consumers at crucial stages of their decision-making process. CDJ will give you an understanding of the role of non-owned marketing, such as editorials, news accounts, or word of mouth. CDJ also allows for a segment-level assessment of touch point effectiveness, using typing tools in the research.

Matching advanced analytical approaches to industries

Some analytical approaches are better suited for certain industries than others. Please note, however, that the advice below is directional rather than deterministic. We encourage you to try out different approaches to find the one that works best for your company.

- **Fast-moving consumer goods**: MMM is recommended because of the high purchase frequency, the strong correlation between investments and sales, and the high availability of weekly or monthly sales data. Note that some consumer goods companies don't have – or at least don't own – consumer sales data ("sell-out"[10]). What they have is sales to retailers and distribution partners ("sell-in"). While sell-in is correlated with sell-out, the buildup of inventory on the intermediary's part and the resulting time delay can inhibit correlation analysis.
- **Retail**: Combine MMM with DA. Typically, MMM works even better for retailers than for consumer goods companies because retailers have direct relations with shoppers – both offline and online – and own the resulting sell-out data. Because most retailers spend an increasing share of their budget on digital marketing, DA is recommended as a secondary approach, especially for those who use multiple digital instruments and find that last-click attribution is not sufficiently precise to single out the impact of individual instruments on sales and other objectives.
- **Consumer durables and automotive**: CDJ is recommended because of the low frequency, long purchase cycles, and multilayered decision-making processes in these industries. Consider DA as an auxiliary approach to fine-tune your investments in digital touch points, especially if the consumer decision journey is very long, involves extended online research, and the first-click contact doesn't typically lead to a sale. This is often the case for high-price items, such as consumer electronics, cars, homes, and some personal finance products.

Use econometric modelling if you have sufficient historical data

Econometric modelling is a well-established, proven approach. Its origins date back to the era of George Gallup, the pioneer of polling, who applied statistical analysis to forecast the outcome of the 1936 US presidential election. In the 1950s, large manufacturers of branded consumer goods – spearheaded by Procter & Gamble – started applying econometric models to marketing investments, driven by the aspiration to make the most of their sizable advertising budgets.[11] This technique employs various types of regression modelling to quantify the statistical correlation of marketing activities with sales or other marketing performance indicators (Exhibit 6.1). It uses historical data – ideally on a weekly or monthly basis – in areas such as sales, advertising investment, competitive advertising intensity, and macroeconomics. The longer the period and the higher the number of data points, the more reliable an econometric marketing mix model will be. Most companies use two to three

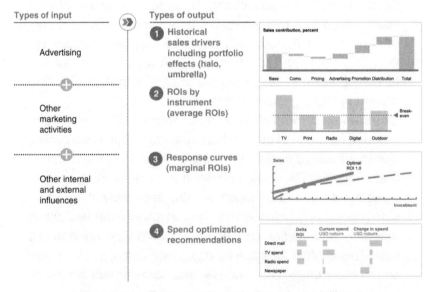

Exhibit 6.1 Econometric marketing mix modelling.
Source: McKinsey

years of weekly data for marketing mix modelling. This is sufficient for very reliable calculations, but leading consumer goods players sometimes use even longer periods. Note, however, that very long periods may bring fundamental changes in market conditions (overall economy, new players in the market, new channels, new tactics) that can be hard to account for.

Econometric modelling is based on the assumption that the future will resemble the past, at least with respect to the purported causal relationships between investment and success. It treats past data series as experiments. Since the intensity of marketing activities changes over time, regression analysis can help estimate the impact of a given activity on the dependent variable, such as sales. Specific benefits include:

- Quantified contribution of individual instruments (e.g., TV advertising, direct marketing, digital display advertising) to sales (or another performance metric). Simply speaking, this tells you which investments in your mix work and which ones don't.
- Calculation of "response curves", i.e., the diminishing return relationship between marketing investment and sales for each instrument. This lets you calculate the marginal ROI of an extra dollar invested in a specific instrument.
- Calculation of real ROI – both average and marginal – for the budget as a whole and for each instrument in your mix. This enables you to treat marketing activities as investments rather than as cost positions.

The output of a state-of-the-art MMM tool helps advertisers separate external factors – such as the overall market growth or demographic trends – from the levers they can address themselves – such as promotional strategy or advertising investment. MMM also provides revenue impact measurements across all marketing levers in order to assess their relative business contribution. Ultimately, MMM provides marketing managers with the means to investigate the likely

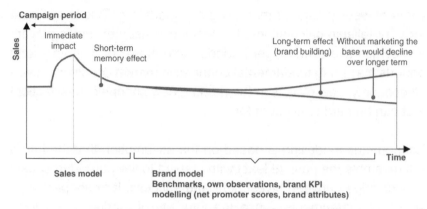

Exhibit 6.2   Short-term and long-term effects.
Source: McKinsey

consequences of their actions before they act, enabling them to make fact-based decisions, instead of relying on intuition.

In theory, econometric modelling is simple enough. If the ROI for a given instrument is higher than one, increase your investment. If it is lower than one, decrease or discontinue your investment. In practice, there are a number of pitfalls you need to steer clear of. A lot of first-time users of econometric modelling focus on short-term sales or new customer acquisition as the dependent variables. This will make instruments that primarily drive brand equity and customer loyalty look bad. So, make sure to integrate indicators of long-term effects as well, such as brand health, net promoter scores, and customer retention, especially if long-term customer relations are a success factor in your industry (Exhibit 6.2). But don't let the complexity get out of hand. Start with the two or three KPIs that matter most.

Of course, getting the input data right is equally important to the reliability of the marketing ROI calculation. Include all relevant marketing instruments in your model – paid, owned, and earned. Econometric models built by media agencies are often limited to paid media – such as TV and print advertising – as influencing factors, simply because these are the only instruments for which they have reliable data. But to reflect the fact that consumers' purchase decisions are influenced by many other factors, econometric marketing mix models also need to incorporate investments in owned media – such as a company's website – as well as the viral effects of social media. In a tragic case of negative online buzz, a company suffered losses exceeding EUR 30 million that could have been avoided by investing less than EUR 1 million in social media marketing. Compare our brochure *Turning buzz into gold*[12] for details.

Finally, a robust econometric marketing mix model should also consider and account for business drivers outside marketing communication, such as new product introductions, pricing, promotions, changes in distribution, interest rate fluctuations, major events, seasonality, holidays, and weather. Sounds complex? It isn't. In fact, it's easy to get started. Most of the data you need to build a basic model is probably already in your system, buried in your media planner's hard drive, or readily available from your media agency. Enlist the services of experts who understand both the essentials of statistics and the principles of marketing and you're good to go.

Apply attribution modelling to the digital instruments in your mix

Digital marketing provides companies with an almost infinite number of new instruments to reach consumers in highly targeted ways. At the same time, it is also a source of massive data on what works and what doesn't work, down to the level of individual users. Digital attribution modelling takes advantage of this wealth of data to help you make the most of your investment in new media. It can also be used to automate decision making in areas such as digital ad buying, using adaptive bid management and ad serving tools. A few advanced players are already managing their entire marketing budget with the help of digital attribution modelling. For others, it is an important building block in holistic marketing ROI optimization. Today, only about 20 percent of marketers use multichannel attribution models that cover all touch points. Some 40 percent use some sort of basic model, such as the attribution of an event to the last click preceding the event, or to the click that started the customer journey. The remaining 40 percent have no attribution model in place at all.[13] Clearly, there is a lot of room for improvement. As a rule of thumb, any company spending 20 percent or more of their marketing budget on digital instruments should look into some form of attribution modelling.

Attribution modelling uses data logged along the digital customer journey – such as ad views, searches on Google, or a click on a link in an e-mail – to determine the contribution of a specific touch point to marketing success (Exhibit 6.3, illustrative). A touch point can be any exposure to marketing communication – be it paid or unpaid – and success can be anything from a sale of a product or a subscription to a service to signing up for a newsletter or registering as a user. Once you understand which touch points have the biggest impact on the things you are trying to achieve in the marketplace, you can increase ROI by shifting investments to those high-impact touch points.

Off-the-shelf online tracking tools – such as Google Analytics or Adobe Analytics – provide a good starting point for attribution modelling. Utilizing a user's last click prior to a desired action – such as a purchase – as a proxy, you can rank competing instruments such

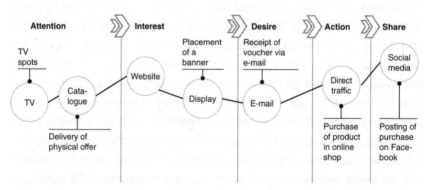

Exhibit 6.3 Contribution of touch points to decision making (illustrative).
Source: McKinsey

as referrals, paid search, and organic search in terms of their relative contribution to your business objectives. Reallocating funds from low-performing instruments to high-performing ones will increase ROI immediately, if only on a small scale. Once you have mastered optimization within a given group of touch points – such as search – you can apply the same principles across different types of instruments, e.g., search engine marketing versus display advertising versus social media marketing. This works best if you compare activities that serve the same objective, such as sales generation. Last click attribution is less insightful if your aim is to compare the impact of different types of campaigns, e.g., awareness creation versus sales stimulation. To keep complexity at bay, respect the 80/20 rule and start by applying attribution modelling to the biggest positions in your digital marketing budget. You can always get more comprehensive and more sophisticated over time (Exhibit 6.4).

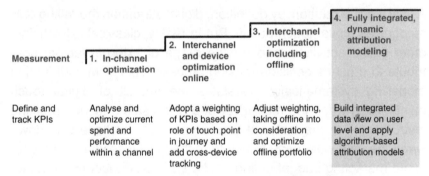

Exhibit 6.4 Degrees of digital analysis sophistication.
Source: McKinsey

Scientific as it sounds, attribution modelling is not actually an exact science – at least not in practice. There are a number of pitfalls you need to watch out for. These include faulty data, misleading dependent variables, and cross-attribution issues. A recorded ad impression, for example, doesn't necessarily mean that the ad in question has actually been seen by the user. The user's attention may have been focused elsewhere on the screen, which is why an ad view is typically defined as an ad that has been displayed for at least one second in the viewed area of a website. Tests show that users often see less than 50 percent of all ads a company pays for. As far as dependent variables are concerned, a lot of specialized tools optimize attribution based on metrics that may not be in synch with your overall attribution logic. For example, bid management tools typically optimize for the price and position of an ad. But if your overall objective is converting considerers to buyers, the tool will skew your marketing mix towards instruments that don't actually do what you want them to do. Finally, it is anything but trivial to connect and weigh the relative contribution of multiple touch points and devices to a given decision journey. For example, a single user may see a YouTube ad on a tablet, then Google the featured product on a laptop, and proceed to make the purchase on a smartphone. Integrating these events into a consistent dataset and ascribing a meaningful contribution to each of them takes experience and expertise.[14]

A final word of caution: by definition, digital attribution modelling only recognizes digital touch points. But in reality, classical advertising, other offline activities, and a wide range of external factors contribute to a user's decision-making process. This is why attribution modelling systematically overstates the impact of digital touch points, even when the real driver of a given sale may be an offline instrument – or the fact that your competitor's website was down when the user was trying to buy from them. Unless you spend your entire marketing budget online, make sure to conduct the required sanity checks and integrate attribution modelling with a more comprehensive approach that covers all instruments, such as Reach-Cost-Quality or econometric modelling.

Consider survey-based approaches – such as consumer decision journey modelling – if you don't have sufficient historical data

Consumer decision journey modelling – or CDJ for short – is based on the assumption that marketing investments are most effective when they reach consumers at the moments that most influence their decisions. CDJ uses consumer surveys to determine what these moments are, and the surveys are designed to recognize the fact that marketing is evolving from proclamation (marketers talking to consumers) towards conversation (consumers talking to each other and providing feedback to companies). Specifically, word of mouth and the recommendations consumers make to their friends feature prominently in state-of-the-art CDJ approaches. This is why CDJ attaches special attention to the post-purchase phase – often referred to as the loyalty loop – in recognition of the need to provide an aftersales experience that inspires loyalty and repeat purchases. This helps marketers ensure that their investments are not overly skewed towards instruments that may trigger short-term sales at the expense of lasting bonds between consumers and brands.

Like the brand purchase funnel discussed in Chapter 3, CDJ is a way of modelling a consumer's decision journey. CDJ models typically work with four primary phases that represent potential battlegrounds where marketers can win or lose: initial consideration; active evaluation, or the process of researching potential purchases; closure, when consumers make a purchase; and post purchase, when consumers experience the product they have bought or the service they have signed up for.[15] More recently, the CDJ model has been updated to account for changes in consumer behaviour, chiefly to account for the fact brands today can not only react to customers as they make purchasing decisions, but also actively shape those decision journeys. Shaping the decision making experience itself with content, interaction, and advice – rather than sending messages to consumers at specific stages of their journeys – is becoming a source of competitive advantage. A recent survey conducted in the US[16] revealed that top performers understood the entire customer journey much better than their peers (20 percent versus 6 percent), and had much better processes for capturing insights about customers and feeding them back into their marketing programmes to improve performance (30 percent versus 11 percent).[17]

Once the contribution of the various milestones along a consumer's decision journey has been determined with the help of standardized surveys, marketers can start optimizing their investments accordingly – for example, by shifting funds from touch points that generate attention to those that help provide customers with a more satisfying aftersales experience. In the past, most marketers consciously chose to focus on either end of the journey – building awareness or generating loyalty among current customers. CDJ enables you to be much more specific about the touch points you use to influence consumers as they move through initial consideration to active evaluation to closure. As a car insurance company, for example, you might want to reduce your investment in advertising and increase your investment in touch points such as claims management to account for the fact that the post-purchase loyalty loop triggers 78 percent of all purchases in this industry (Exhibit 6.5).

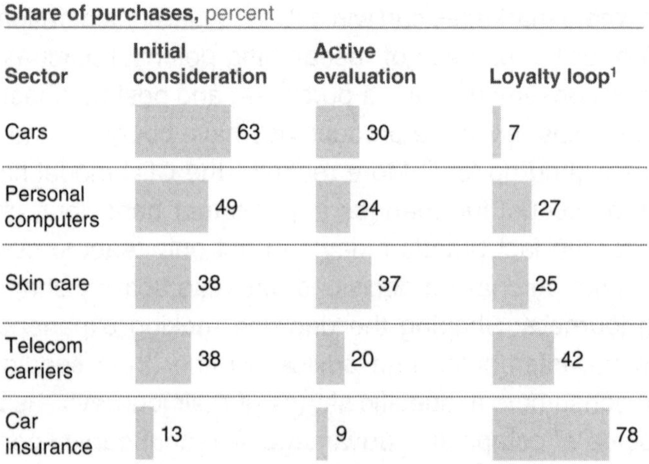

Share of purchases, percent

Sector	Initial consideration	Active evaluation	Loyalty loop[1]
Cars	63	30	7
Personal computers	49	24	27
Skin care	38	37	25
Telecom carriers	38	20	42
Car insurance	13	9	78

1 Consumers who purchased the same brand without shopping other brands

Exhibit 6.5 Number of brands added for consideration in different stages by industry.

Source: McKinsey consumer decision surveys

The principal advantage of survey-based approaches is that they work without historical data. So if you don't have sufficient data on past investments and sales, or have reason to doubt its reliability and consistency, CDJ is a great alternative to assess the relative contribution of touch points to marketing success. The limitation of CDJ is twofold: any survey-based approach is just a snapshot derived from an observation at a single moment in time and it depends on the reliability of consumers' self-knowledge as far as the stated importance of specific milestones and experiences along their decision journey is concerned. For the latest thinking on new sources and techniques to compensate for these limitations, compare our upcoming publication on the future of insights.[18]

Build a hierarchy of analytical approaches to avoid conflicting results

Many providers of advanced analytics will tell you that their approach – be it econometric, attribution-driven, or survey-based – can help you manage your entire marketing budget. In our experience, that is rarely true. There is no single approach that works irrespective of which industry you are in, what your marketing mix is like, and how much data you have. At the other end of the spectrum, there is an almost infinite number of highly specialized solutions that will let you optimize a handful of touch points – or a single one – to a tee, but neglect the bigger question of roughly how much you should be spending on that particular instrument to begin with. In either case, you will create considerable complexity, produce inconsistent results, and miss out on part of the opportunity. What is even more important, there is high risk of frustrating your team and confusing your fellow executives with a myriad of metrics and conflicting recommendations.

To avoid this, we encourage you to establish a clear hierarchy of analytical approaches and pick your battles wisely. For example, the head of marketing for a global retailer, thrilled by the lure of big data and the prospect of scientific precision, spent months on attribution modelling to optimize the tiny fraction of the budget that was actually dedicated to digital response marketing, such as online vouchers. At the same time, the millions that went into old-school promotions and local leaflets were woefully neglected. As the CMO, you owe it to yourself and to your organization to approach mix optimization systematically, and to focus your attention on the biggest opportunities. In our experience, econometric modelling works best to determine the appropriate high-level mix between offline and online instruments. If you don't have sufficient data, you may want to use Reach-Cost-Quality (see last chapter) or survey-based models instead. Once you have established this overall frame of reference, you should try out more sophisticated techniques to optimize key instruments within the bigger buckets, such as attribution modelling, to determine the most effective touch points for search engine marketing.

And even if you have all the data in the world, don't feel like you have to go for the most sophisticated models on the market right away. If your organization isn't ready for data-driven decision making, you may end up wasting money and frustrating your team. Compared with manual mix decisions, even simple models can bring efficiency improvements of up to 20 percent. Don't buy a Ferrari if a Fiat can do the job.

Application example: TV advertising for a telecoms player

While many companies use advanced analytics to optimize the marketing mix across multiple instruments, the same methodology can also be applied to the options within a single channel, such as television advertising. In a given case, a telecoms player used econometric modelling to determine which time slots, channels, and sellers provide the best contact-to-ad spend ratio in their target group for television advertising. Based on econometric modelling that linked the number of gross new subscribers to advertising spending, the company decided to move its television advertising from prime time (after 7:30 p.m.) to pre-prime-time slots (6:30 p.m. to 7:30 p.m.). Additionally, they switched to an advertising sales house with higher effective discounts. As a result of these efforts, the company increased the return on its television advertising investment by more than 60 percent without compromising brand awareness or advertising recall. For details on the optimization of individual instruments, see the next chapter.

Key takeaways

- Pick an analytics approach that fits your business situation in terms of purchase frequency, ticket prices, and data availability.
- Use econometric modelling if you have sufficient historical data to determine the contribution of past investments to past successes.
- Apply attribution modelling to the digital instruments in your mix, especially if you invest a substantial share of your budget in digital marketing.
- Consider survey-based approaches – such as consumer decision journey modelling – if you don't have sufficient historical data.
- Build a clear hierarchy of analytical approaches to avoid conflicting results, starting with a robust model to inform top-level allocation.

NOTES

1. http://searchengineland.com/google-1-trillion-searches-per-year-212940; 2014.
2. http://www.broadbandchoices.co.uk/guides/broadband/guide-to-internet-data-usage, 2014.

3. A touch point is any one opportunity for an individual to make contact with an advertiser's message, e.g., a TV commercial, an online video, a print ad, an online banner, a billboard, or a sponsored search result.

4. http://blog.performics.com/the-importance-of-multi-touch-attribution-an-illustration/.

5. http://www.international-television.org/tv_market_data/.

6. Compare the upcoming McKinsey white paper on *New Insights for New Growth*, by Jonathan Gordon, Volker Grüntges, Vicki Smith, and Yvonne Staack, due for publication in early 2016.

7. emarketer 2015.

8. An instrument is a group of touch points, such as "search" (comprising search engine marketing and search engine optimization) or "display" (comprising various forms of online ads, such as banners or pop-ups).

9. Attribution is the ascription of an effect to a touch point. If multiple touch points are involved in a purchase decision, attribution will help quantify the relative impact of each of these touch points on the decision.

10. In most developed markets, consumer goods companies can get weekly sales data at the SKU and store level from providers such as Nielsen. In developing markets, companies may need to use sell-in as a proxy of sell-out.

11. For details, compare *The History of Marketing Science*, by Scott A. Neslin and Russell S. Winer, WSPC, Singapore, 2015, and http://thedoublethink.com/2009/07/history-of-scientific-marketing/ (retrieved in December 2015). Also compare Paul Feldwick, "The four ages of ad evaluation," Admap paper, April 1996. In the 1980s, OHAL, now part of Gain Theory, was among the pioneers of econometric marketing mix modelling.

12. Available through the authors of this book.

13. Webmarketing123, "2015 State of Digital Marketing," February 10, 2015.

14. So-called "device-graph" companies, such as Tapad, specialize in matching multiple devices to a single user based on cross-device usage patterns, but there is no well-established mechanism at this point.

15. http://www.mckinsey.com/insights/marketing_sales/the_consumer_decision_journey.

16. Association of National Advertisers. The survey was completed by a total of 384 marketers. Participants comprise members of various panels, including the Association of National Advertiser's (ANA) Marketer's Edge Research Community, ANA members and prospects, the American Marketing Association, Demand Metric, McKinsey, and Spencer Stuart. Findings from the survey will be available in "The marketer strikes back," forthcoming on the McKinsey on Marketing & Sales website.

17. http://www.mckinsey.com/insights/marketing_sales/the_new_consumer_decision_journey.

18. Volker Grüntges et al., "The end of the survey? New insights for new growth" (working title, McKinsey Q1/2016).

7 – SMART ACTIVATION

Trim the fat off key instruments to drive incremental benefit

Why does smart activation matter?

In 2014, US federal agencies spent USD 1.8 billion on printing. Simply by changing the standard font used in government documents to Garamond, the Government Printing Office could save as much as USD 400 million – the equivalent of 22 percent of the total printing budget – without even reducing the font size. This is because Garamond – a typeface that has been in use for almost 500 years and is the most popular font for book printing today – needs less ink than, for example, Century Gothic and other fonts recommended or commonly used by federal agencies. The change would not impair legibility in any way, and the USD 400 million estimate does not even include environmental benefits.[1] Have we got your attention?

Effective activation is crucial to make sure brand messages and marketing campaigns get through to your target group. But why waste precious funds on a fancy font, overpriced TV channels, the wrong shows, ineffective online search terms, or leaflets half the recipients don't even look at? You can't afford any of that if you want the marketing department to act as a profit centre, rather than being a cost position. Some of the world's most experienced marketers are already doing it. Says P&G's CMO Mark Pritchard: "What makes this spending so difficult to manage is that it's a combination of thousands of activities. However, that's also what gives us confidence we can achieve significant savings by approaching this more systemically. Simply shining the light on wasteful spending can cut costs of some of these elements literally in half."[2]

The US printing example might sound very specific, and that is exactly what makes smart activation so challenging. Who knows off the top of their head what the equivalent of a change in typeface might be for rich media ads or point-of-sale materials? Let's face it, there is no single lever you can pull to trim the waste across all media. The drivers of efficient activation are very specific to the different instruments in your mix. Also, de-specification is not exactly the most exciting part of marketing. But the opportunity is substantial. P&G, for example, hopes to reduce its USD 14 billion marketing budget by USD 1 billion without sacrificing consumer impact.[3] Imagine what you could do with that kind of money: run an experimental cross-media campaign, try out a new instrument, hire a Hollywood director to mastermind your next viral clip, or fund the brand campaign that always got bumped off the list in the past. As the CMO, you don't have to deal with the particulars, but you should encourage your team and your agencies to put their sourcing on a healthy and nutritious diet – the kind that gives your brand exactly what it needs. Establish and enforce the principles of smart activation and you will soon see a leaner, more efficient marketing budget emerging, freeing up funds you can invest elsewhere more profitably.

How to drive marketing performance with de-specification

There are dozens of marketing instruments, and you can't be world class in all of them. Unfortunately, it's easy to get caught up in secondary theatres of war. Consider the case of the brick-and-mortar retailer that neglected old-school leaflets for the sake of digital marketing excellence mentioned in the last chapter.[4] The trick is to focus on the instruments that drive your business and absorb the bulk of your budget. For companies that depend on strong brands – such as most consumer goods companies – this is usually still classical advertising, notably TV commercials. However, some advertisers deliberately choose to go against the grain and aspire to own a less obvious instrument. IBM, for example, reinvented out-of-home advertising for its "Smart ideas for smarter cities" initiative. The campaign included the installation of branded structures, such as rain shelters and ramps, that actually improve people's lives.[5] Similarly, Red Bull has long focused on event marketing and owned media; compare our insert in Chapter 4. For offline retailers, local marketing is a big deal and absorbs up to 70 percent of all spending. Even if this share is declining for them, leaflets definitely deserve close scrutiny and optimization. After all, every euro you save by trimming the specifications for dominant, traditional instruments frees up funds for new activities.

In contrast, digital instruments are paramount for companies that depend chiefly on transactions, especially in highly price-sensitive areas. Examples include travel, energy, and e-commerce. Companies in these industries often spend a significant share of their budget online – be it to ensure high ranks on comparison portals such as Kayak, or to generate click-throughs to their offering from Google results pages. So pick the instruments that are make or break for your company, build in-house competence in these areas – at least to a degree that enables you to challenge your agency's recommendations – and seek out expert help to cut the waste. In some cases, you will need advanced analytical techniques, such as the ones presented in the previous chapter. In other instances, case studies and benchmarking will help you make the relevant trade-offs. Apply the same principles one level down. Within digital marketing, for example, determine the most relevant types of websites – portals, content aggregators, or social media sites – before you consider investments in specific ones. If you monitor for consumer impact and let agencies participate in your savings, de-specification is pretty much a risk-free exercise – provided you are clear about who your target group is and what you are trying to achieve in the marketplace. Compare the Introduction and Chapter 1 for details on objective setting.

Adopt an incremental benefit mindset and be prepared to kill your darlings – even if it hurts

Pick an instrument. Any instrument. Ask yourself: What did I get for the last euro I spent on this instrument? Was it worth it? Could I put it to better work by changing the specifications within the instrument, e.g., by placing an ad in another environment? The amount you paid for a full-page print ad, for example, might have bought you two half-page ads that would have generated a higher net reach with the same or only marginally lower campaign recall rates. Similarly, the amount you paid for a plain banner ad on a premium website might be worth several rich media ads placed at a less prominent destination. Ask yourself: Would it be worth trading the obvious choice for another option? In a second step, apply the same thinking across instruments: What if I didn't produce a TV commercial next season? The savings on creation, production, and activation could easily amount to the funds you need for half a dozen YouTube clips, a spectacular local marketing campaign, or a sponsorship engagement.

Adopting an incremental benefit mindset means submitting all your activities to the same sober scrutiny: What do I get for my money? What if I invested one more euro? What would it buy me? Would it be worth it? Of course, more is usually better, but how much better? Could we achieve higher impact by investing that extra euro elsewhere? In other words, how does the incremental return compare with the alternatives? There will always be reasons to defend a given investment because of its average impact, or simply because it feels like something you should be doing. What self-respecting brand doesn't run a high-profile mass media campaign before Christmas?

Forget the average and forget the sacred cows. Do the math. Calculate, for example, what it cost you to achieve that last percentage point of penetration in your target group. Was it money well spent? If the incremental benefits are slim, consider decreasing your investment in one instrument – or a specific activation pattern – and trying something else instead.

In what follows, we will apply the concept of incremental benefit to three crucial instrument types: classical advertising, digital marketing, and direct campaigns. Please note that our aspiration is to provide you with examples that will inspire your own optimization efforts in these areas, rather than to embark on a holistic treatment of each group of instruments.

Consider the road less travelled by and seek out efficient niches in mass media

TV is a notoriously noisy environment. There are hundreds of channels and thousands of shows. All major advertisers are clamouring for the most prestigious slots, such as Black Friday or the Super Bowl halftime show. Industry observers say that the cost of airing a 30-second ad in this kind of environment may soon hit the 10 million dollar mark, more than the entire marketing budget of many medium-sized companies.[6] In Latin America, a provider of personal financial services found itself in a spending battle with competitors to secure coveted prime-time spots for 30-second commercials, generating dozens of opportunities to see the same spot for their target audience, much more than the company's marketing objectives would have required – and well beyond meaningful incremental returns in terms of additional recall or likeability. There is nothing wrong with securing sufficient share of voice, but don't let competitors' wasteful practices entice you to overspend in turn.

In a given case, a leading multibrand consumer goods player set out to streamline its investment in TV advertising. The company was spending 50 percent of its total media budget on television. In a stagnating market, the cost per second was increasing at a rate of about 15 percent annually. Overall mix guidelines were already in place, but the optimization of individual instruments had not yet been addressed. After extensive research and analysis, the company made three principal changes to its TV investment:

- Lower reach targets. An analysis of incremental cost per TRP (target rating point) revealed that the last few percentage points of reach were disproportionately expensive. For new campaigns, the average unit cost for each of the last three percentage points (65 to 68 percent) was more than twice as high as that of the base (up to 65 percent). For promotional campaigns, the difference was even more dramatic. The final few percentage points of reach were more than four times as expensive as the base. In response, the company reduced its reach target by 2 percentage points. This de-specification helped cut the TV media budget by more than 10 percent.
- Shorter spots. The share of short spots (15 seconds) was increased at the expense of longer spots (20 and 25 seconds). According to independent research, short spots are almost as effective as long spots. Across countries, 15-second spots reach 78 to 97 percent of the effectiveness of 30-second spots in terms of a combination of metrics such as attention, recall, brand attribution, and likeability (Exhibit 7.1). The company decided to generate 30 to 50 percent of total reach through short spots, and use longer spots almost exclusively during the early stages of a campaign. These changes added up to savings of 9 percent of TV media cost.
- More effective ad break positions. The company opted not only for shorter spots, but also for less costly positions for these spots, moving them from the end of the ad break to its beginning (first or second slot, instead of last or second to last). Although the last slot is typically the most coveted, the numbers don't bear out this preference. Because many viewers only return after the end of an

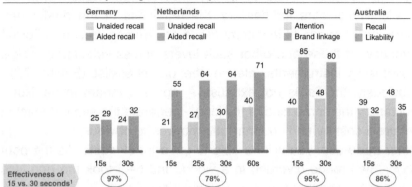

Exhibit 7.1   Effectiveness of short TV spots versus long TV spots.
Source: Psyma, SevenOne Media; University of Tilburg; *Journal of Consumer Research*; Ameritest; Nielsen Media Research; Kantar; *Journal of Advertising Research*; press clippings

ad break, the number of viewers is below the median for this slot. In contrast, first and second positions typically reach an above-median viewership (13 percent and 5 percent respectively). This change resulted in about 1 percent cost savings for the advertiser.

Additionally, the company reduced the number of its weekday morning spots for its drinks and dinner brands and booked more evening positions instead. The objective was to move the communication closer to the consumption occasion and increase the ROI through higher impact on consumer behaviour. Finally, the advertiser invested in a tracking tool that helps the media team monitor and adjust advertising intensity and spending patterns almost in real time. In total, the savings reached a magnitude of 25 percent of the company's TV media buying budget without compromising consumer impact.

In another case, a Chinese car manufacturer drove up return on classical advertising spending dramatically, mainly by synchronizing air times of campaigns for new models with the availability of cars for delivery, the readiness of the dealer network, and periods of low competitive advertising pressure. For an overview of these and other such levers across selected classical advertising instruments, please see our checklist (Exhibit 7.2).[7] Obviously, the list is not exhaustive, nor is it meant to be. But if you apply the same kind of thinking – generate the same impact at reduced cost by finding smart alternatives to obvious choices – to other trade-offs, you will be able to cut a lot of waste. As the poet says: "Two roads diverged in a wood, and I – I took the one less traveled by, and that has made all the difference."[8]

Break the average in digital marketing and focus on the keywords and inroads that drive your business

Half of all digital ad spend goes to search engine marketing (SEM).[9] If you spend anything on digital marketing, chances are it will be on search engine optimization or advertising, and this is also the one channel that you need to get right in terms of smart activation. You can easily waste millions by having your messages displayed to users who couldn't care less, or by trying to outbid your competitors for the same half-dozen search terms. Do you really need to claim the most popular keywords? And should you invest in the same keywords all the time? Of course, digital marketing goes well beyond search engines. While SEM still accounts for at least half the budget in many industries, other online media types are catching up. According to industry observers, each of the following instruments accounts for budget shares of up to 25 percent:[10]

- Display/video advertising
- Referral from other sites
- Outbound e-mail and newsletters.

We encourage CMOs to take an active interest in driving the return on their investments in digital instruments. Consider the case of a

	Execution lever	Key analysis
	Spot length	Incremental recall/brand impact vs. cost per second
	Share of prime-time vs. day and night time	Incremental reach vs. incremental cost
	Share of prime month/week vs. non-prime month/week	Incremental reach vs. incremental cost
	Share of prime day vs. non-prime day	Incremental reach vs. incremental cost
TV	Share of first/second and last/penultimate position in ad break	Cost per reach in incremental percentage point of reach
	Overall penetration of target group	Cost per reach in incremental percentage point of reach
	Average frequency of contact/ opportunity to see (OTS)	Incremental recall/brand impact vs. cost/OTS
	Target choice of channels: national vs. regional vs. local TV	Average cost per view increase and cost per second vs. incremental recall/brand impact
	Size of ad (full page vs. half page)	Incremental increase in time spent on page shared with other content vs. incremental recall/brand impact of larger ad vs. incremental cost of ad
	Improve position (C2 vs. C4, left vs. right)	Incremental recall/brand impact vs. incremental cost of ad
	Target choice of format (insert, banderole, etc.)	Incremental recall/brand impact vs. incremental cost of ad
Print	Target choice of media type (newspaper, magazine, etc.)	Target group reach vs. incremental cost of ad
	Share of prime day vs. non-prime day	Incremental recall/brand impact vs. incremental cost of ad
	Quality of creatives (targeted, color, etc.)	Additional cost vs. incremental recall/brand impact
	Target choice of format (billboard, public transport)	Target group reach vs. incremental cost of ad
Out of home	Size	Incremental recall/brand impact vs. incremental cost of ad
	Target choice of position (location, lighting, etc.)	Target group reach and incremental recall/brand impact vs. incremental cost of ad

Exhibit 7.2 Typical levers to optimize activation of classic media instruments.

Source: McKinsey

leading European online transaction platform that reaches some ten million users per month in more than a dozen countries. Inspired by best practices observed in other categories and industries, the company submitted the biggest positions in its multimillion euro digital marketing budget to systematic scrutiny. The objective of the effort was to identify and eradicate inefficiencies in individual instruments to drive the return on marketing investment. Examples of improvements include:

- SEM keyword portfolio streamlining. The keyword portfolio used for search engine advertising was reviewed systematically to determine incremental contributions, down to the profitability of each keyword. The company quickly discovered that it was too costly to own generic keywords, such as "marketplace", at least in developed markets. In response, some funds were shifted from a small number of generic keywords to a long tail of less popular keywords because these were found to yield a better return on investment in this case. In addition, ads and landing pages for high-value keywords were refined to increase conversion rates. As a result, the cost per click decreased by up to 20 percent, and the cost per lead went down by as much as 40 percent. As part of the effort, the company also reviewed its overall keyword strategy based on a simple question: Which searches have the biggest potential to generate revenues? Today, the list of keywords the company bids for in automated auctions is reviewed and adjusted on a daily basis.
- Affiliate marketing revision. The company generates a lot of leads through referrals from affiliated partners – such as comparison sites, content aggregators, and blogs. As part of a de-specification effort, all such partners were screened with regard to the return on investment (cost per lead). Cooperation agreements with low-performing partners were discontinued. New incentives were put in place – such as tiered bonuses for leads exceeding the contractual agreement. The company also devised clear guidelines for all affiliates – especially regarding the integration of ads into the partner's offering – and now keeps a blacklist of repeat violators.

As a result, the average cost per lead went down by 24 percent. Because of this jump in efficiency, the company ended up shifting funds from other instruments to affiliate marketing.

- Outbound e-mail optimization. Benchmarking revealed that the portal's e-mail-driven traffic was below the industry average, and that leading players generated up to five times as much traffic through outbound e-mail. Taking inspiration from best practices, the company engaged in systematic A/B testing of different targeting approaches. At any one time, thousands of slightly different e-mail campaigns were in progress. For example, e-mails to repeat visitors might include a link to a category that the customer has researched before, while known bargain hunters might receive alerts to special deals. Some variations were much more subtle, such as different colours for a key visual. In addition, the company introduced frequency caps to make sure a unique user doesn't receive more than a prespecified number of e-mails in a given time period. As a result of these efforts, click-through rates increased by 26 percent.

- Display ad fine-tuning. The company conducted a simple experiment with display ads. The actual banner was displayed only in half the ad spaces the company had paid for, while the other half was deliberately left blank. This test revealed that as many as 70 percent of all ads were ineffective, partly because they were served outside the viewable screen area. In response, the company renegotiated contract terms and included incentives to reward ad sellers for incremental traffic. As a result, the cost per click for certain ads went down by 40 percent.

In total, the de-specification effort resulted in savings of 20 percent of the online marketing budget without decreases in traffic or revenues. The biggest mindset change was to move from hypothesis-driven marketing (doing what you think might work) to data-driven marketing (doing what is proven to work). Currently, the company is looking into shifting funds from SEA to SEO. There is some indication that SEO might eventually replace all SEA. But further tests are required, and the company will have to invest in proprietary content around major traffic-driving categories.

As this example shows, there is a lot of room for improvement in the way individual digital instruments are used. Please see Exhibit 7.3 for an overview of some smart activation levers for a range of digital instruments, from search engines to social marketing.[11]

Digital marketing is a very dynamic environment. As new technology becomes available, new opportunities for arbitrage are bound to arise. Be prepared to test new solutions quickly and measure their impact on your marketing objectives – and don't hesitate to stop using them if they are not working. If you don't, your budget will inflate in all the wrong places.

Experiment with different combinations of distribution, frequency, sequencing, and specifications for direct marketing activities

In theory, direct marketing is immune to waste. By definition, direct marketing messages are only sent to members of your target group, and you only expose them to messages you consider relevant for them in light of their needs and preferences. In practice, there is still significant potential for optimization. Start by putting yourself in the shoes of your target customers: What do they really care about? What are they indifferent to? And what are the things that really bother them? Before long, you will come up with changes to your direct marketing specifications that will spare your customers undue disturbance and save your company a lot of money.

In many markets, leaflets are still the most important marketing instrument for brick-and-mortar retailers. In a given case, leaflets accounted for more than 60 percent of total marketing spending at a European retailer. Traditionally, distribution areas were chosen based on ZIP codes, with each ZIP code comprising thousands of households.[12] An initial cross-analysis of leaflet distribution and shopper data gathered at the checkout revealed that

	Execution lever	Key analysis
Search engine optimi- zation (SEO)	Invest in long-tail non-brand keywords	Cost per reach and cost per action (CPA) vs. SEM cost per click (CPC) alternative on non-brand keywords
	Secure top organic ranking in brand keywords	Cost per reach and CPA vs. SEM CPC alternative on brand keywords
	Implement technical prerequisites	Additional effort and cost of development vs. incremental visits and click through rate (CTR)
	Invest in targeted landing pages	Additional effort and cost of production and development vs. incremental visits and CTR
Search engine marketing (SEM)	Reduce dependency on paid search compared with organic reach	CPC and CPA vs. SEO reach on relevant keywords and potential SEO investment
	Focus on conversion vs. reach/branding	Total conversions vs. total clicks
	Increase positioning vis-à-vis competitors	Incremental effort and average CPC increase vs. incremental market share and visits increase
	Keyword targeting: broad match vs. exact vs. phrase	Average CPC increase vs. incremental clicks
	Device uptake/elimination	Additional effort and cost of development vs. incremental reach (visit and conversion) and CPA reduction
	Increase targeting (time of day, location, month, etc.)	Incremental reach (visits and CTR) vs. average CPC increase
	Invest in targeted landing pages	Additional effort and cost of production and development vs. incremental reach (visits and CTR) and CPA reduction
Display	Programmatic vs. premium	Average CPM/CPC vs. brand impact, visits, and conversions
	Retargeting uptake/elimination	Additional effort and cost (including average CPC increase) vs. incremental visits and conversions and CPA reduction
	Reduce frequency of ads	Incremental brand impact and visits vs. average CPA and CPC increase (beware of "over-delivery" curve)
	Increase quality and differentiation of creatives	Additional effort and cost of production (including average CPC and CPA increase) vs. incremental brand impact, visits, and CTR (CPA reduction)
	Device uptake/elimination	Additional effort and cost of development vs. incremental brand impact, visits, and CTR (CPA reduction)
	Uptake of new partners/networks	Additional effort of contact and CPC/CPM vs. incremental brand impact, visits, and CTR (CPA reduction)
	Increase targeting activities (e.g., location, context, etc.)	Incremental average CPC and CPA increase vs. incremental brand impact, visits, and CTR (CPA reduction)
Video	Programmatic vs. premium	Average CPM vs. performance increase
	Increase targeting of creatives according to platform	Incremental effort and cost of production vs. incremental brand impact, visits, and CTR (CPA reduction)
	Reduce spot length	Incremental recall/brand impact vs. cost per second/CPC
Paid social	Broad targeting vs. specific targeting	Incremental cost vs. Incremental brand impact, visits, and CTR increase (CPA reduction)
	Broad creative vs. specific creatives	Incremental effort and cost of production vs. incremental brand impact, visits, and CTR increase (CPA reduction)
Affiliate	Network vs. premium	Average CPA vs. brand impact, visits, and conversions
	Reduce inclusion of coupons	Incremental cost of cost per conversion vs. increase in conversions and conversions per reach

Exhibit 7.3 Typical levers to optimize activation of digital instruments.
Source: McKinsey

20 percent of all leaflets went to postal codes that generated only 2 percent of revenues. To reduce scatter losses, the retailer conducted regression analysis to identify the real drivers behind revenues generated by leaflets: driving distance to the closest store, purchasing power, and household size. Based on these indicators, the company defined new distribution microclusters of no more than 50 households each. The company used McKinsey's Local Media Excellence (LoMEX) geomarketing tool to adjust the leaflet budget, optimize the selection of distribution areas, standardize the decision process, and generate reports. The leaflet budget was reduced by 15 percent, and profits increased by 1.5 to 5 percent, depending on the performance of individual stores.[13] In a similar fashion, IKEA reports that geomarketing has helped the company cut the circulation of their catalogue by 500,000 copies in Germany alone.[14]

Here are some thought starters for similar de-specification opportunities in other areas of direct marketing:

- Do you need to deploy multiple direct instruments? If yes, should you use them in parallel or in sequence to maximize the impact? For example, assume a user frequently clicks on links in your electronic newsletter or e-mail messages. Do you really need to send that same person a letter as well? If yes, when is the best time for the mailing? Channel preference modelling will help you determine the best instrument – or combination of instruments – for every single user.[15]
- Do you need to start your campaign with the costliest instruments? Best-practice players establish initial contact through instruments that generate high reach at low cost before deploying more expensive instruments. A personal finance company, for example, started their acquisition campaign by sending e-mails to a long list of prospective new customers. In a second wave, those who had responded to an e-mail received an outbound call. Only customers who had expressed serious interest in a call centre conversation were eventually contacted by a sales rep in person.

- Can you piggyback on inbound calls or other service interactions? Outbound calls are a nuisance for many people. Why not use an existing interaction – such as a customer's inbound call – for upselling or cross-selling instead? Insurance companies, for example, do it as part of claims management. You should also consider enriching transactional communication, such as a bill or a sales confirmation by e-mail, with direct marketing messages. This creates little to no additional cost, and your message will reach customers in a situation in which they are already tuned to your company.
- Do you need glossy paper and full colour for your catalogue? Do these features help trigger higher purchase frequency or bigger basket sizes? To find out if they do, conduct a real-life test. Send a simpler version of the catalogue to a predefined group of customers and closely monitor the impact relative to recipients of the high-end catalogue. Perhaps you can inflect your mailing according to customer value: restrict the full, glossy version to A and B customers and send a plain ten-pager in black and white to C, D, and E customers. You'll be surprised by how small things like these add up to substantial savings. The cost-cutting potential can amount to as much as 20 percent of total cost.

See Exhibit 7.4 for an overview of smart execution levers and typical trade-offs for various other direct marketing instruments.

Make a habit of evidence-based activation planning and establish golden rules – both across and within individual instruments

Smart activation is as much a mindset as it is a process. Don't think that you can go through one round of de-specification and be done with it. While you are busy streamlining classical media planning, chances are that one of your well-intentioned fellow board members is about to sign off on a new sponsorship deal without asking the big questions: Does your target group care about it? Will the features of the event drive your business objectives?

	Execution lever	Key analysis
Outbound	Channel preference (letter, telephone, or e-mail)	Incremental reach and targeted reach (leverage cost-efficient e-mail for reach and use telephone and/or letter contact for hot leads) vs. incremental cost per contact
	Reduced frequency	Incremental reach vs. incremental cost per contact (beware "over-delivery" curve/frequency cap)
Inbound	Reduced size of inbound force	Incremental reach and targeted reach (all calls should have purpose of generating conversions) vs. incremental cost per contact (compare with cost of reach via website)
Leaflets	Reduced paper quality (page finish, paper grade, number of colours, binding, etc.)	Incremental reach/brand impact vs. incremental cost of production per leaflet
	A/B testing at scale	Additional effort and cost vs. incremental reach and conversions
	Reduced length of leaflet	Incremental reach/brand impact vs. incremental cost of production per leaflet
	Reduced inclusion of coupons in leaflets	Incremental cost of production per leaflet and cost per conversion vs. increase in conversions and conversions per reach

Exhibit 7.4 Typical levers to optimize activation of direct marketing instruments.

Source: McKinsey

And do the licence fees leave enough wiggle room for activation? Does the investment promise appropriate returns? Make a habit of challenging both new deals and current activation practices from an incremental benefit perspective. Ask for evidence that supports the specifications of all major marketing activities. If in doubt, don't hesitate to commission additional research to find out whether a premium placement, a rich media ad, or a glossy mailing are worth the added expense, or whether less costly alternatives have the same effect. Control group tests should be a matter of course for your team to assess alternative specifications, especially for online advertising and direct media that allow you to measure the effect on a single user basis. Don't tackle all topics at once, though. Focus on the big buckets, and keep checking back on practices that were state of the art three years ago. Chances are that things will have changed. Try something new, even if it feels like a long shot. Take a chance to fail on a small scale in order to win big eventually. And don't hesitate to stop doing things that don't work – or don't compare favourably with alternative investments – even if it hurts.

As you get more experienced, start compiling smart activation guidelines for key instruments. Draw on your own experience, lessons learned from past campaigns and tests, the expertise of your team and your agencies, and relevant industry best practices. While these rules will typically be specific to each given instrument, some golden rules apply across the board. Examples include:

- Don't sign off on a premium ad placement – be it offline or online – unless there is a clear and plausible business case to support it.
- Always get a second opinion on the activation plan for a major campaign, ideally from an independent media planning auditor.
- Employ advanced analytics to narrow down the target group for a given campaign; for example, with channel preference or next-product-to-buy (NPTB) modelling.
- Only pay for what your predefined target audience actually gets to see, hear, or experience – especially online.
- Before you green-light a new creative idea, testimonial, or spon-sorship deal, check whether you could make more of your existing assets.

Key takeaways

- Adopt an incremental benefit mindset and be prepared to kill your darlings – even if it hurts.
- Consider the road less travelled by and seek out efficient niches in mass media.
- Break the average in digital marketing and focus on the keywords and inroads that drive your business.

- Experiment with different combinations of distribution, frequency, sequence, and specifications for direct marketing activities.
- Make a habit of evidence-based activation planning and establish golden rules – both across and within individual instruments.

NOTES

1. Suvir Mirchandani and Peter Pinko, "A Simple Printing Solution to Aid Deficit Reduction", *Journal of Emerging Investigators*, March 6, 2014.
2. http://www.warc.com/Mobile/News.aspx?ID=30653 (retrieved December 7, 2015).
3. http://www.campaignasia.com/Article/291772,PG+chief+lays+out+$1+bill ion+marketing+efficiency+vision.aspx (retrieved December 24, 2015).
4. In the case in question, the company focused on digital instruments that were the talk of the town at the time, and because detailed metrics were available for these instruments. But they failed to acknowledge that leaflets still absorbed a large share of their budget and drove a lot of business, despite a slow decline in importance.
5. http://www.trendreports.com/article/out-of-home-advertising.
6. http://www.forbes.com/sites/alexkonrad/2013/02/02/even-with-record-pric es-10-million-spot/.
7. For further reading, we recommend *AdMap* magazine, as well as articles and reports published by agencies such as MillwardBrown, media owners such as SevenOneMedia, and trade associations such as IPA, WFA, or OWM.
8. Robert Frost, "The Road Not Taken" (http://www.poetryfoundation.org/ poem/173536).
9. Magna 2015.
10. Based on international traffic tracking by SimilarWeb (2015).
11. For the latest news, we recommend the following resources, last retrieved in February 2016: https://moz.com/rand/; https://searchenginewatch.com/; https://googleblog.blogspot.com/; http://www.kaushik.net/avinash/. For a comprehensive account, please see Avinash Kaushik, *Web Analytics 2.0: The Art of Online Accountability and Science of Customer Centricity*, Sybex, 2009.
12. According to the December 2015 census, a US ZIP code is home to a population of 7,592 on average (http://www.zip-codes.com/zip-code -statistics.asp, retrieved December 23, 2015).
13. For a detailed description of this case, as well as a more comprehensive discussion of local marketing excellence, see Chapter 14 of *Retail Marketing and Branding*, by Jesko Perrey and Dennis Spillecke, Second Edition, John Wiley & Sons, 2013.

14. *Der Handel* 09, September 2, 2009, p. 24.
15. Compare *Change the Channel: A New Multitouch Point Portfolio*, by Paul-Louis Caylar et al., McKinsey, 2014. (http://www.mckinsey.com/~/media/mckinsey/dotcom/client_service/Telecoms/PDFs/February%202015%20-%20Recall%20papers/Change_the_channel_2014-08.ashx). .

8 – PARTNERS

Build performance partnerships with marketing service providers

Why do partners matter?

So you're the CMO. Do you want the CFO to tell the CEO that he is doing your job? Then don't read this chapter. Because sooner or later, the procurement department will review all vendor relations for your entire company. Chances are that the bloodhounds will dig up dozens, if not hundreds, of contracts with marketing service providers. Some of these vendors you will not even have heard of. Others – such as your lead creative agency – will be important partners that help you build your brand and drive marketing performance. In any case, the CFO will have a field day sorting you out. You don't want that? Then read this chapter.

"I want the kind of research that lets me see inside the consumer's head." – "We need someone to track our brand in social media." – "Let's run the best campaign money can buy." As a CMO, you will have heard this rap before, probably from your CEO, or even the supervisory board. If only it were so easy. What do you do yourself, and what do you pay others to do for you? How do you select service providers? And how do you make sure that they do what you depend on them to do – and do it well? How do you keep them hungry, and how often do you check on them? Last but not least, how do you keep third parties from besting you, or charging you for services you never signed up for?

Marketers today depend on the support of an entire ecosystem of third-party providers, from research firms and creative agencies to media planners and online marketing specialists. In fact, the bulk of pretty much any marketing budget is spent on external vendors rather than on internal resources. Marketing services have evolved into an industry in its own right, generating revenues in excess of a trillion US dollars (2013, Exhibit 8.1). In the US alone, there are more than 100,000 advertising agencies.[1]

And while digital technology is making the lives of marketers easier in many ways, it also has given rise to various kinds of "marketing

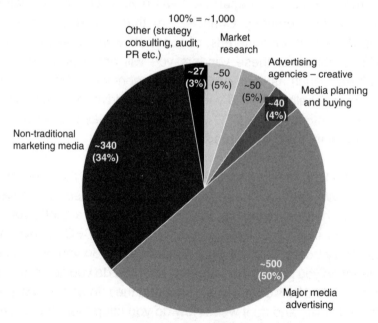

Exhibit 8.1 The market for marketing services.
Sources: AdAge, BMO report, IBIS World, GWA, Kennedy, press research, McKinsey

technology" providers that constitute an entire subsystem of service providers:

- *Enablers of marketing services*, such as mobile, social, or content marketing players.
- *Marketing operations specialists*, offering data gathering, data mining, analytics, and programmatic buying.
- *Providers of technological infrastructure*, such as data management, customer relationship management (CRM), cloud hosting, and mobile app development.

Industry observers, like marketing tech blogger Scott Brinker, list almost 4,000 solutions in these areas,[2] and new ones are launched every day.

Picking the right partners from this vast and complex array of players and managing them well will enable you to drive both the "R" and the "I" in marketing ROI. The return – or the effectiveness of your efforts – will benefit from superior creative services, sophisticated media plans, and early adoption of relevant technological innovations. And managing the providers of these services well, both during contract negotiations and performance reviews, helps to keep the "I" – or the cost – at bay. A high-performing ecosystem of service providers will make sure you get the best the market has to offer, and it gives you the flexibility to take advantage of new opportunities as they arise. If you observe the ground rules laid out below, you will have nothing to worry about when the CFO mounts a vendor review.

How to drive marketing performance through service provider management

Managing marketing service providers is not a onetime effort, but a continuous process. To get it right, you have to keep asking the same set of questions again and again: In which areas do we need third-party support? How should our portfolio of service providers be set up? In each of the functional areas, who are the right partners? How can we ensure we get good value from them for the money? And how can we form performance partnerships that make sure that everybody wins if our brand thrives?

Keep strategic control in-house

Are all marketers lazybones? We don't think so, but the degree of outsourcing is remarkably high in marketing. In a recent study, marketers said that most functions are almost "fully outsourced", including sensitive areas such as media strategy development[3] (Exhibit 8.2). There is nothing wrong with hiring someone to provide specialized services. But the functions that drive value creation at your company should be the privilege of your own managers, and

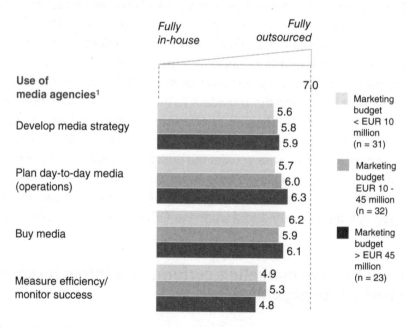

1 Average on a scale from 1 = "work is done fully in-house" to 7 = "fully outsourced"

Exhibit 8.2   Degree of marketing outsourcing by service type.
Sources: OWM and McKinsey

some non-core functions call for checks and balances to make sure agencies and advertisers are pulling together.

Whatever you do, don't let any vendor control your marketing strategy. The brand identity and value proposition belong in the hands of your senior executives, as do decisions about long-term marketing and communications strategy. In recognition of this principle, some companies have taken deliberate action to insource core tasks. As Jonathan Mildenhall, a senior marketer at Coca-Cola at the time, once put it: "Coke had to take creativity in the widest sense back from the agencies. It couldn't belong only to the hairy elites of agency creative departments."[4]

On the other hand, third parties bring the experience, the scale, and the speed that come from working across many companies and industries. So do not hesitate to take advantage of external specialists in non-strategic areas. Internal capability building takes a long time, can be very costly, and it makes you inflexible as consumer needs and communication channels evolve. What's more, chances are your team will never reach the proficiency of outside specialists in certain fields, such as marketing technology. We will discuss the benefits and the pitfalls of marketing technology solutions in more detail in the next chapter. Some functions, however, come with a built-in conflict of interest between the company and its vendors. Take media planning. The media plan that is best for the agency is not necessarily best for the advertiser. While the agency seeks to maximize its profits, the advertiser wants the mix of media, choice of titles, and levels of activation that best support its marketing objectives. There is widespread concern among advertisers regarding the transparency and legitimacy of media buying conditions. So great is their worry that the American Advertising Association has launched a large-scale project to review the practices in this area.[5]

So keep strategic marketing in-house, enlist the services of third parties in non-core areas, and always make sure your team has the expertise to review and challenge the recommendations of outside service providers.

Rebuild your portfolio from scratch

Have you heard of GMOOT? It's a disease, and it's highly contagious. GMOOT is short for "Get me one of those", and third-party management is highly susceptible to it. Someone high up in the corporate hierarchy, or some whiz kid straight out of college, has seen a tweet about a cool piece of software, heard a rumour about the latest fad in mobile marketing, or been to an event hosted by a hot boutique agency. Before you know it, you have entered contractual agreements with three new service providers you may or may not have use for. And sooner or later, they will start messing with your brand. You don't need that.

Don't enslave yourself or your brand to what other people think you should be buying in. As the CMO, you have the best sense of the jobs that really matter, whether you need outside help to get them done, and which vendors are best suited to complement the capabilities of your own team. Take control of your portfolio, and make sure you balance quality (the best agency for each job) with complexity (a reasonable number of agencies in total). Don't start with your current roster of service providers. Instead, take stock of what you really need. We call this the "zero-based" approach, and it has helped many of our clients clean up their portfolios, reduce transaction costs, and drive efficiency.

Start by mapping out the types of work you will need to do over the course of the next few years, e.g., campaign development, media planning, digital marketing, and so on. Then determine how much agency support you need in each of these areas. As you do this, think about the requirements of different brands, countries, and business units in your company. Some services – such as marketing technology – can be sourced centrally and rolled out globally, whereas others – such as media planning or PR – depend on local agency presence and expertise. And while some services – such as web hosting or sourcing of physical materials – can be easily bundled, others – such as sponsoring or retail marketing – call for case-by-case decisions.

It can be a cumbersome effort, but when you are done, you will have a robust list of what you really need, including the types of service providers, as well as the scale and scope of services. You will be surprised by how short and how helpful that list will be. At least that is what major global advertisers felt when they did the exercise. Examples include Unilever, L'Oréal SA, and Visa. Most prominently, Procter & Gamble announced in 2015 that it was planning to reduce the number of advertising agencies it works with dramatically.[6] But before you start hiring and firing, set aside some time to weigh the pros and cons of different portfolio structures (Exhibit 8.3).

Keep your eyes open

If you had gone into cryonic sleep five years ago and woke up today, you wouldn't recognize the agency landscape. It was already highly fragmented in 2010, and new players have entered the scene virtually every day since. Entirely new functions have emerged, while others have gone out of style. At the same time, some sectors have seen rapid consolidation. Smaller players are being sucked up by a handful of conglomerates, or forced out of the market altogether. The advertising industry, for example, is already dominated by four giants: WPP PLC, Omnicom, Publicis, and the Interpublic Group. Collectively, these four groups generate some USD 50 billion in annual revenues.[7]

So, how do you stay on top of this complex, rapidly evolving provider market? There is nothing wrong with traditional sources of information, such as trade journals, industry newsletters, agency

	Description	Pros	Cons	Implications
One integrated agency	One agency hired to perform all services within existing agency	• Integration • Customer management time • Discounts	• Rare one agency can do it all • Lacks best-in-class	• Believe in efficiency vs. best-in-class trade-off
Custom agency	Holding co. creates custom agency	• Great integration • Efficient client management	• Talent acquisition/retention	• Work harder to retain talent
Leader among holding company siblings	One agency hired to perform all services, all from same holding company	• Streamlined accountability • Resource flexibility • Integration • Discounts	• Some limits on best-in-class • Less flexibility with conflicts	• Believe holding company resources are good enough
Lead agency	One agency "leads" overall brand and helps manage/coordinate across agencies	• Tight client-agency coordination • Potentially integration	• Tight coordination • Integration • Animosity between agencies	• Need proof agency can integrate • Brands "cede" some control
Multiple best-in-class	Multiple agencies hired across disciplines; customer coordinates	• Resource flexibility • Ensures best-in-class	• Increased customer management time • Integration	• Requires robust central marketing services • Brands need to integrate ideas
Free agent	Customer draws from multiple/varying agencies as needed	• Ultimate flexibility	• Integration "free for all" • Lacks partnership	• Project mentality • Slow ramp-up • Brands need to integrate

Exhibit 8.3 Types of agency models.

Source: McKinsey

rankings, industry conventions, and creative awards ceremonies. Leading players have even established an executive position to stay on top of the vendor landscape.[8]

Unilever has taken a slightly different approach. To identify the best marketing technology start-ups, the company has created the

"Unilever Foundry", a platform for collaboration with promising start-ups. Real briefings are posted online, and every start-up that thinks their product or service may fit the bill can submit a proposal. Based on a preselection of five to six companies, Unilever brand managers choose a provider for a pilot. This entire process often takes no more than two months. It has resulted, for example, in a collaboration with a technology start-up based in South Africa. The company helped Unilever create a text-based service needed to reach users of old-school mobile phones in sub-Saharan Africa, where smartphones were virtually unknown at the time. Text-based marketing turned out to be a powerful driver of consumer engagement, and Unilever has since rolled it out to other areas.[9] Other companies are spreading a certain sliver of their agency funds even more thinly, e.g., by holding open competitions and giving a test budget to a comparatively high number of agencies.

Your company is not ready for a sourcing platform or an open competition? Then why not join forces with the CFO and have the procurement department screen the vendor landscape for you? Some companies even have established dedicated marketing procurement specialists, sometimes with a dotted line to the CMO. But don't make a habit of having agencies pitch for your account all the time – least of all in strategic areas. And don't let the total number of marketing service providers get out of hand. Performance partnerships require a measure of continuity and trust to prosper. You don't want a new agency messing with your brand every other year. Consistent messaging is a key prerequisite of sustainable marketing performance.[10]

Do your homework

Bring down the price of external services, and the "R" as a percentage of the "I" in marketing ROI automatically goes up. It's as simple as that. But this very simplicity may be what keeps companies from pursuing contractual negotiations as the powerful driver of marketing ROI that they are. The plain fractional arithmetic of "R" over "I" just doesn't sound nearly as sexy as the multivariate regression analysis that is often involved in mix optimization (see Chapter 6). Don't get us wrong. We are not saying you should not engage in advanced analytics. You should. But you should also ensure you are getting your money's worth from service providers, the way any sober tradesman would.

Supplier management can generate 10 to 15 percent in savings without sacrificing marketing impact (the "R" in marketing ROI). In essence, supplier management is about paying less for what you buy, i.e., reducing prices without changing the specifications of products purchased and services rendered. Admittedly, specifications in marketing are harder to pin down than in more tangible areas, such as raw materials or prefabricated components. How do you define the required level of quality – let alone creativity – for an advertising agency? It takes a lot of expertise, experience, and care to make sure you don't cut corners where it really matters. But such challenges should not stop companies from managing marketing investments with the same rigour as other investments. Proven tactics include:

- *Bundling volume*: Buying from fewer service providers enables you to capture volume discounts. Relevant cost positions include creative agency services, production services, media agency services, media buying, and marketing technology. Volumes can be bundled across legal entities, business units, departments, brands, regions, and countries.
- *Switching to providers that give you better value for money*: Items such as POS material or giveaways can often be purchased more cheaply from providers in low-cost countries (so-called LCC sourcing). Try to pick countries in which your company has a branch or subsidiary so you can have someone go check on low-cost providers for quality management and compliance with ethical and environmental standards.

- *Negotiating rigorously*: It may sound trivial, but if you come well prepared and are willing to see things through, chances are you will be able to get better service for what you're paying, cut commissions, or extend payment terms. Make sure you are included in all relevant negotiations, e.g., when media agencies sit down with media owners to work out rates and kickbacks. Many companies have not done this, and they are paying dearly.

Keep in mind that certain functions – such as creative services – are crucial to marketing value creation and should be optimized for quality rather than cost. Switching creative agencies is a big deal. The last thing you need is new people trying reinvent your brand every other year. The downside of losing the expertise and experience of a trusted partner may easily outweigh the savings you hope to capture from hiring a cheaper competitor, or from forcing your agency to scale down the size or the seniority of the account team by driving for lower rates. To hedge this risk, build a mixed portfolio of agencies and assign them different roles. For example, put a top agency in charge of creating the big ideas for your campaigns and work with a flexible roster of high-quality second-tier agencies to develop local adaptations.

Be a great client

What do you do when your million-dollar campaign tanks? You blame the creative agency. What do you do when brand equity nosedives? You fire the market research firm. What do you do when the website crashes? You pin it on the digital marketing contractor. When things go wrong, it's always someone else's fault. It's a natural reaction, but you know it isn't true. We are all for accountability, but it should be a two-way street.

There are a number of things you can do to be a great client. It starts with a good briefing. Make sure service providers know what you expect from them by establishing clear objectives for a given campaign or activity. Investing time in a good briefing initially will give you the confidence to let the agency do their thing later on. Many companies underinvest in clear briefings and overinvest in pestering service providers with follow-on discussions when what they need most is the freedom to innovate and create. Who exactly is the target group, what do we know about them, and what is the change in attitude or behaviour that we are trying to achieve? Sometimes it can be as simple as making clear who gets to sign off on the agency's work throughout the development process. We have seen many campaigns go downhill because the agency didn't know who was in charge on the client side. Trying to please everyone is bound to produce a result nobody likes. Think of the briefing as the bridge between strategy and creation, and make sure that it provides your contractors with all the insights and objectives they need to do great work (Exhibit 8.4).

And when great work is done, do not hesitate to acknowledge it publicly and reward it financially. Performance-based fees are a great way to bring out the best in service providers. Don't think of this as a cost-saving mechanism. You want great work, and if you get it, the return it generates enables you to pay for it. However, the classic agency compensation model – a commission fee on media or production cost – has many disadvantages. Not only does it incite agencies to favour "expensive" media over potentially more efficient or innovative instruments; it also gives you, the client, an incentive to cut back on upfront planning and keep requesting reworks, simply because they come at no additional cost. The traditional commission is going out of style anyway. According to an ANA[11] survey, 61 percent of companies in the US use performance incentives. Most players (69 percent) use a combination of client and agency performance. Popular indicators include agency performance review scores (75 percent), advertising awareness (54 percent), and client sales (48 percent). Leading multibrand players pay agencies a percentage of total sales or value generated by all brands that are part of the agency's account. Depending on the strategic importance

Project description

☐ What is the exact task the agency is expected to perform (creative, media plan, ...)? Details on the project (e.g., 1x30 second TV commercial to launch campaign X)

☐ What is the scope of the work (media to be used, copy lengths, timing, and duration of the campaign)?

☐ What is the business opportunity/challenge (context within which the objectives are set)?

☐ What criteria will be used to assess the agency's performance?

Background

☐ Where is the business now?

☐ What is the context of the campaign (e.g., strategic relevance)? Why action is needed?

☐ What competitors are relevant in this context?

☐ What customer insights are available/should be taken into account? What behaviour change is required?

Campaign objectives

Communication objectives

☐ What message do we want to convey (benefit, reason why)?

☐ Which indicators/KPIs will we use to measure the campaign's success?
  ☐ Brand funnel performance (e.g., awareness, sales, or loyalty)
  ☐ Brand attribute perception (e.g., on "trust")
  ☐ Other

Target group

☐ Who is our target group? What do consumers currently think, feel, and do?

☐ Is the communication target group a different one?

☐ Which consumer segments should be targeted (e.g., security-minded, price-sensitive, convenience-oriented, ...)?

☐ What do you want them to take away after experiencing the communication?

Brand proposition

☐ What are the key elements of the brand proposition (real drivers of choice)?

☐ What are brand differentiators and brand personality/tone? (Attach any brand positioning statements/documents or key support that details the proposition, especially in relation to competitors)

Requirements

☐ Are there any practical considerations (e.g., taglines, properties to use, etc), legal mandatories, and/or any other executional mandatories to take into account? – Keep it brief

Execution

☐ Are there any specifics on execution or creatives?

☐ Are regional differences going to be considered?

Frame conditions

☐ What is the maximum cost and time frame (budget for the actual project, estimate of media to be used, types of channels)?

☐ What are the payment conditions (e.g., success-dependent, linked with communication objectives)?

Exhibit 8.4   Elements of a good briefing and key questions to address.
Source: McKinsey

and prospective value of a given project, agencies will receive a bonus of up to 30 percent if they hit predefined impact targets.[12] In a perfect world, your team and your agencies work towards the same set of targets and are rewarded based on the same performance indicators, ideally with marketing ROI as the master KPI. There is nothing more frustrating than conflicting objectives, and nothing more motivating than a common cause. Trust us, even the CFO will agree.

Key takeaways

- Keep strategic control in-house. Be mindful of what you outsource, and make sure your team has the expertise to challenge the recommendations of external experts.
- Rebuild your portfolio from scratch. Take stock of what you really need and resist buying some service or solution just because the CEO thinks it's fashionable.
- Keep your eyes open. Don't wait for vendors to come to you. Actively screen the service provider landscape and try out new players and approaches.
- Do your homework. Commission fees and payment terms are powerful drivers of marketing ROI, so get your ducks in a row prior to negotiations with third parties.
- Be a great client. Accountability is a two-way street. Create an environment in which service providers are inspired and incentivized to do great work.

NOTES

1. http://www.agencyspotter.com (retrieved in December 2015).
2. http://chiefmartec.com/2016/03/marketing-technology-landscape-supergraphic-2016/ (retrieved in March 2016).
3. http://www.wuv.de/marketing/studie_marketer_haben_keine_ahnung; survey conducted in 2012 (retrieved in December 2015).
4. http://digiday.com/agencies/pulsepointes-5-reasons-brands-cutting-agencies/ (retrieved in December 2015).

5. http://www.adweek.com/news/advertising-branding/ana-launch-fact-findin g-probe-media-buying-kickback-claims-165290 (retrieved in December 2015).

6. http://www.wsj.com/articles/p-g-joins-movement-to-cut-ad-costs-1430093 596; http://adage.com/article/ad-age-research/p-g-cuts-agencies-40-wave -consolidation/299750/ (retrieved in December 2015).

7. http://www.nytimes.com/2016/03/19/business/j-walter-thompson-gets- new-chief-after-departure-over-suit.html (retrieved in March 2016).

8. "Agency of the future," McKinsey report, June 2013.

9. https://foundry.unilever.com/unilever-foundry-and-lions-innovation-launch- search-for-worlds-top-50-marketing-technology-startups (retrieved in December 2015).

10. Compare the discussion of consistency in Chapter 1.2, as well as the discussion of agency pitches in Chapter 4.6 of *PowerBrands – Measuring, Making, and Managing Brand Success*, by Tjark Freundt, Jesko Perrey, and Dennis Spillecke, Third Edition, Wiley, 2015.

11. Association of National Advertisers, 2013. For details, compare the discussion of agency payment practices in Chapter 4.6 of *PowerBrands – Measuring, Making, and Managing Brand Success*, by Tjark Freundt, Jesko Perrey, and Dennis Spillecke, Third Edition, Wiley, 2015.

12. "Agency of the future," McKinsey report, June 2013.

9 – IT SOLUTIONS

Use marketing ROI decision support solutions to transform your company

Why do IT solutions matter?

Give someone a fish, and you feed them for a day. Teach someone how to fish, and you feed them for a lifetime. Moses Maimonides, the Jewish philosopher, coined this saying almost a thousand years ago in reference to acts of charity, but it is no less applicable to corporate conduct today. Sure, you can buy a fish, but why not buy a fishing rod instead? As a marketing executive, you can pay a specialist to optimize your mix of instruments and budget allocation, employing the methods and tools outlined in the preceding chapters. Nothing wrong with that. But the impact of any such effort will be restricted to a few budgetary cycles at best. Things change, people move on to new roles, and knowledge is lost. Little by little, gut feeling and rules of thumb creep back in. Then what? Hire another service provider to set things straight again? Not a great idea for a number of reasons. You will be sacrificing marketing ROI between rounds of optimization. You will create the impression that you need constant outside help to do your job. You will be wasting money on service providers that you should be spending to build your brand. The CFO will have a field day dishing the dirt on you. You don't need any of that.

An integrated marketing ROI solution will not only help you stay in control. It also buys you time. Manual data gathering, integration, and analysis take forever. And despite the best efforts of your team, any manual approach will only be relevant for one planning cycle. Next year, they will have to do it all over again to account for new input data and new parameters. Frustrating? You bet. A state-of-the-art IT package, however, automatically integrates new data from a variety of sources as it becomes available, and it makes insightful analyses easily accessible to decision makers – not once, but continuously. It also puts an end to infinite cycles of cumbersome auditing. Once the input data is validated at the source, an integrated solution ensures that all downstream calculations benefit from the original quality control.

You think you can do the necessary calculations on the back of an envelope? Think again. State-of-the-art mix optimization relies heavily on big data and advanced analytics. In other words, you will need IT support anyway, even for a one-off effort. So why not make it permanent? Why not put in place a sustainable solution that allows you to revisit previous optimization cycles on a regular basis? You will be much less susceptible to changes in corporate strategy, industry dynamics, competitor action, regulation, consumer behaviour, and instrument availability. Time and again, you will be able to adjust your marketing mix, using the sources and algorithms that went into the original effort. With the right kind of tool, you will even be able to make real-time adjustments as a given campaign proceeds. Testing and learning will be much easier, and much faster, than before, and the things you learn will help refine your decision support system. Once people start working with the tool continuously, the kind of thinking it is based on will become common knowledge and help enhance the capabilities of your team and the agencies you work with.

In addition, professional IT-enabled marketing ROI solutions will also help you cash in on scale. Many companies engage in optimization efforts with very limited scope initially – e.g., limited to one of several business units, one of many brands, or one of dozens of countries. Even if they plan to roll out the approach to other parts of their business, they often get stuck somewhere along the way. A stand-alone solution may not be as universally compatible as the vendor had promised, or the in-house team may lack the skills to make it work with new parameters and data sources. In fact, even the impact of a pilot can quickly dwindle without ongoing IT support. In our experience, companies that embed marketing ROI optimization into their IT systems are more likely to maintain and even grow the impact than those who don't (Exhibit 9.1). So go for an integrated, scalable solution that is designed to work in a wide variety of environments, and you will have a much easier time in sustaining the impact and multiplying the benefits of an optimization by applying it across your company.

In short, we recommend you get yourself a fishing rod.

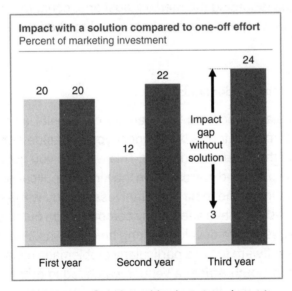

Impact with a solution compared to one-off effort
Percent of marketing investment

First year: 20, 20
Second year: 12, 22
Third year: 3, 24

Impact gap without solution

Exhibit 9.1 Solutions drive long-term impact.
Source: McKinsey

How to drive marketing performance through IT solutions

Of course, you can try making that fishing rod yourself. But since you're not in the software development business, why bother? In any case, it would take a long time and tie up your team when they should really be building the brand. Yet the outcome will probably be inferior to professional solutions. There are plenty of specialized vendors out there, and there is a high probability that one of the existing packages will work for you. And even if a given solution isn't 100 percent right, it can often be customized to your specific requirements. Your job is to specify what those requirements are to meet your decision needs – and to make sure the solution you choose is sufficiently integrated with your business. If that is the case, an IT solution will work as an insurance that protects you from costly mistakes – namely investments in irrelevant or inefficient instruments. Frequent updates will help you keep your marketing mix in synch with changes regarding the media landscape, consumer behaviour, competitor moves, and the latest analytical methodologies.

Take stock of the vendor landscape

Before you start specifying your requirements – let alone select a vendor or a specific tool – we suggest you set aside some time to take stock of the vendor landscape. This will help you get a sense of the solution space and narrow down the kind of application that suits your needs. One of the most important lessons you will learn is what you *don't* need. We have seen many companies go out and buy software packages or hire developers long before it was clear what they needed the software for. In a particularly problematic case at a major corporation in South Africa, a vendor was hired to automate a marketing ROI algorithm that turned out to be inherently flawed. Even the finest IT implementation of the methodology the company was using would have produced misleading results – a textbook case of garbage in, garbage out. For this company, the challenge was not to find the right IT solution, but to pressure-test and refine their methodology first. This is something technology-minded service providers will rarely be able to do. So, as you talk to vendors, try to get a sense of whether they understand what you are trying to achieve with the tool and whether they have the necessary marketing and business expertise.

As indicated in the previous chapter, there are three principal categories of IT vendors that cater to marketing professionals: enablers of marketing services (or "experiences"), marketing operations players, and providers of technological infrastructure. The infrastructure category can be further subdivided into middleware, backbone platforms, and supporting tools, such as database solutions and app development packages. A combination of vendors across these layers will form the "technology stack" that suits the needs of your company.

- *Enablers of marketing services.* These are providers of tools and applications that help marketers reach and interact with consumers in new ways. Examples include mobile marketing, display advertising, video marketing, search advertising, community and review management, e-mail marketing, influencer marketing, social media marketing, search engine optimization (SEO), and content marketing.
- *Marketing operations specialists.* These companies support marketers in their efforts to make sense of consumer needs and improve the effectiveness of their marketing mix. Examples include data gathering, data management, data mining, analytics, tag management, and cloud computing. Most marketing ROI solutions, such as Market Share or the McKinsey Marketing Navigator, fall into this category.
- *Providers of technological infrastructure.* These service providers work behind the scenes to make digital operations easier for marketing professionals and their partners. Broadly defined,

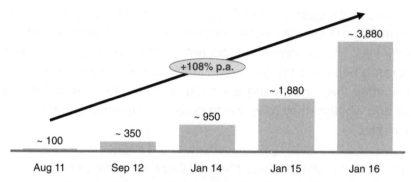

Exhibit 9.2 Number of marketing technology companies.
Source: Scott Brinker, chiefmartec.com.

infrastructure ranges from middleware to backbone platforms, such as CRM solutions, e-commerce applications, and developer tools. Leading providers in this area include IBM, Oracle, and Adobe.

Within each of these categories, dozens – if not hundreds – of companies are competing for the attention and the budget of corporate marketers, and their number is still growing (Exhibit 9.2). Before you request proposals from any of them, narrow down your requirements as much as possible, starting with a solution that will help you make better, more informed decisions about how you spend your marketing dollars on a regular basis. Don't hesitate to enlist the services of a vendor management specialist to help you develop the respective briefing and preselect relevant service providers. Says Gayla Sullivan, a research director at Gartner: "Vendor management is increasingly important as a distinct discipline because newer models and niche vendors can generate a lot of value for a business, while also introducing a high degree of risk that requires management."[1] Keep in mind that a simple solution can often deliver more value than a high-end package. You don't need an armada of fishing boats when all you want to do is catch a trout for dinner.

Specify realistic requirements

Form follows function. This principle, originally established by architect Louis Sullivan, also applies to IT architecture. So before you start ogling some award-winning CRM solution, or that fancy-looking marketing ROI dashboard everybody was talking about at the last CMO summit, take a step back and ask yourself: Which business questions do you need the IT solution to answer? Do you just want to track brand equity, or do you need a sophisticated solution that lets you model the impact of different mix and allocation scenarios on long-term marketing ROI? Do you need something that works for a single country, or a system that supports decisions across multiple regions and subsidiaries? Make sure you pick a solution that fits the organizational structure of your company and its processes, or at least one that can be customized accordingly. In some companies, major marketing decisions are reached at an international business unit or brand management level, and then broken down into marketing plans for individual countries. In other companies, it's the other way round: marketing decision making happens nationally and is consolidated into an international framework only at a later stage. The IT solution you choose to optimize marketing ROI should reflect the way things are done at your company. Otherwise, the software will not be perceived as helpful by your staff, and they won't use it.

So, before you even start talking to prospective vendors, talk to your team. Make sure you understand what an IT solution should deliver to make their lives easier within the context of your company's strategic priorities. Do they need a tool to determine the overall budget level, or to allocate a given budget to different investment units and instruments? Which investment units and marketing vehicles will it have to incorporate (see Chapter 2)? Should it only help them make more informed budgeting decisions, or should it also contain a module that supports brand message definition (see Chapter 3)? You want the modules and features of an IT solution to match the operational model of your company, the core processes of your marketing department, and your strategic priorities.

Once you move into the design phase, simplicity and ease of use are key. A lot of IT solutions are rotting on some forgotten server because they are too complex, or lack user-friendly interfaces to existing systems. A state-of-the-art marketing budgeting tool should be compatible both with the most important data sources – such as the reports of your default research provider – and with the desired output – such as the budgeting module of an enterprise resource planning (ERP) suite. If marketers have to pull, transfer, transform, reformat, upload, and export data manually all the time, they will quickly get frustrated and stop using the solution in question. And even if they don't, any data-driven process that involves too many manual steps is prone to error and inaccuracy. NASA famously lost a USD 125 million space probe because of a unit conversion error. "This is so dumb," John Logsdon of the space policy institute at George Washington University said at the time.[2] Don't let the same thing happen to your marketing ROI solution.

Transparency is another requirement. Nobody wants a black box. This was always true for software applications used in a corporate context, but it has become an even bigger issue over the course of the past decade. The growing number of data sources, brand touch points, and competing marketing mix models have given rise to ever more complex solutions. In many cases, these tools produce recommendations without revealing the specific reasons why, or even the general principles they are based on. Attribution modelling (see Chapter 6) can skew mix recommendations towards digital touch points by exaggerating the efficiency of digital marketing, caused by a lack of data for offline touch points. This systematic error frequently goes uncorrected, or it creates conflicts with more traditional econometric modelling. In either case, black box allocation algorithms shatter marketers' trust in IT solutions, and often in fact-based marketing ROI optimization in general.

If in doubt, pick a less sophisticated tool that – figuratively speaking – lets you peer over its shoulder, rather than a rocket-science solution nobody understands. Before you buy any package, have the vendor explain in detail how it works, and have your team challenge any built-in assumptions. As a general rule, we encourage you to learn to drive before you fly. Even small additions to your arsenal of tools can make a big difference to the way your team works with data. Start with a simple dashboard that gives you an overview of key marketing performance indicators. Encourage your team to observe and report how investments in different campaigns and instruments affect those indicators and to optimize the marketing plan in light of such insights. Before you know it, evidence-based decision making will become the new normal, and there will be no shortage of ideas for upgrades to your suite of solutions.

Application example: Media spend optimization in electronics retail

Consider the case of a multibillion dollar electronics chain. Traffic and same-store sales[3] had been declining for years. The retailer's media spend had traditionally been focused on newspaper inserts and television. There was little to no digital marketing. Additionally, the company's ad-to-sales ratio was higher than that of its competitors, resulting in below-average profitability. The retailer was under pressure from investors to cut its marketing spend without putting sales at risk.

The company opted for a marketing ROI solution that supported very granular media mix modelling. Marginal ROI was quantified for a wide range of allocation scenarios for different markets, product categories, and periods. The recommended reallocation was tested in multiple markets, refined, and eventually rolled out to the entire network. As a side benefit, the model helped the marketing team pinpoint a number of tactical improvement opportunities. For example, both distribution of printed materials and the mix of 15-second TV and 30-second TV ads were optimized. Savings from these tactical improvements were reinvested to expand the company's digital footprint.

In the end, the company was able to reduce its media spend from USD 160 million to USD 140 million, the equivalent of 12.5 percent in savings. Sales not only remained stable, but actually grew by USD 50 million annually, largely due to continuous application of the marketing ROI tool once the original optimization effort had concluded.

The tool used in this case was McKinsey's Marketing Navigator,[4] a solution that integrates a variety of analytical approaches (e.g., Reach-Cost-Quality, marketing mix modelling, and digital attribution modelling). The Marketing Navigator comprises four modules:

- The *Value Navigator* helps you determine the optimal budget size and allocation in light of a given strategy, business objectives, and market opportunities (see Chapter 2).
- The *Brand Navigator* uses purchase funnel performance and brand driver analysis to define the most effective messages for a given target group (see Chapter 3).
- The *Mix Navigator* provides the fact base for an optimal mix of specific touch points in the context of a given budget, using the one currency approach (see Chapter 5).

- The *Campaign Navigator* comprises guidelines and best practices for superior execution in terms of demand, supply, and process management (see Chapter 7).

Solutions such as the McKinsey Marketing Navigator (Exhibit 9.3) typically help companies save 15 to 20 percent of marketing spending without sacrificing market impact, or reallocate funds to support new growth. Other innovative providers include Marketo for B2C companies, Demandbase for B2B companies, and ThriveHive for small and medium-sized enterprises.[5]

Business questions	Tool at hand	
Allocation *Where to spend?*	Tool to optimize your allocation	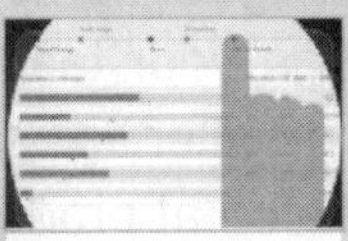
Message *What to say?*	Tool to tailor message	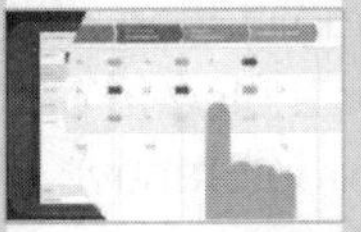
Mix *How to connect?*	Tool to optimize mix	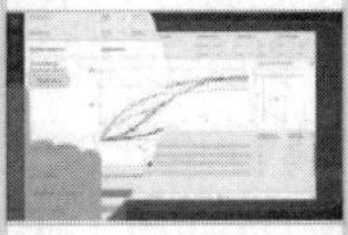
Execution *Which way to execute?*	Tool to plan campaign	
Sustainable impact *How to drive change?*	Integrated solution	

Exhibit 9.3   Tools tailored to business question.
Source: McKinsey

Get the ball rolling

A fishing rod helps you catch fish. In fact, catching fish with a rod is much easier than catching fish with your bare hands, as anyone who has tried (and doesn't happen to be a polar bear) will readily confirm. Yet catching fish is only the most obvious use of a fishing rod. Put a rod in someone's hand, show them the ropes, and you will change their lives forever. There's a number of things you can do to make sure a marketing ROI solution doesn't just help you capture substantial savings, but transforms your team along the way.

It starts with the setup of the tool itself. Obviously, you want it configured to calculate all the standard marketing KPIs your company works with – from brand equity and purchase funnel performance to full-fledged marketing ROI. But the right numbers aren't enough to engage your team, let alone your fellow board members, with their short attention spans and even shorter tempers. Pick a tool that doesn't stop at producing sound numbers, but also provides coherent visualization of the output. If the tool itself doesn't support that, look for a plug-in or custom add-on. There is nothing more powerful than an interactive interface that lets you experience the impact of your decisions in real time. For example, some tools provide slide controls that users can play with to twist and tweak the budget level and media mix. In another window, or on a second screen, a dynamic diagram shows how such changes affect reach, cost, and ultimately incremental ROI. Ideally, find a tool that also lets you build, save, and modify different scenarios. Export some of those scenarios to PowerPoint, and your next board presentation will practically run itself. Some McKinsey Marketing Navigator users even utilize the tool itself to discuss marketing plans with the CEO.

In-house communication in general is a key success factor to make the impact of marketing ROI optimization stick and grow your reputation as a data-driven manager. Talk to your fellow executives before you even request proposals from vendors. Include a wide circle of senior executives – from marketing and sales to IT and finance – and encourage them to share both their success stories and pain points, and be sure to include their perspective in the briefing. Once the new solution is in place, spread the word about how it helps the company make more informed decisions and unlock new growth. Much like any other product, a marketing ROI tool will not sell itself. You of all people should know this. So be aware of your internal target group, explore their needs, and make sure to demonstrate how the tool makes their lives easier and contributes to better business.

When it comes to your own team, make sure they embrace the effort from day one, from development and testing to implementation and daily operations. Once the tool is in place, we recommend a "field and forum" approach, i.e., a combination of classroom training interspersed with periods of fieldwork. Assign staff members real-life tasks that require them to use the new tool, and have them convene periodically to share their experiences. This will help build and preserve marketing ROI capabilities throughout your organization, well beyond the narrow circle of experts involved in the original effort. Pilot users of the tool can be powerful advocates. Even if they formally report to other department heads, let them know you consider them your allies and encourage them to talk about how data-driven marketing is changing their work experience and the company for the better. If funds are restricted or time is tight, start with a single business unit, brand, or country to demonstrate the impact. Before you know it, others will be standing in line to become a part of what you are doing.

Create a legacy

Good IT solutions will help you capture long-term benefits, but they need your foresight and attention to take effect. We encourage you to use IT solutions to make marketing ROI optimization an integral part of how you run the marketing department – the data you gather, the metrics you look at, the trade-offs you consider, and the decisions you make. Invest in process definition: Who is responsible for data gathering, validation, and entry? How often do they need to update the input data? To what degree can updates be automated? Is there an interface for other corporate functions – such as the finance departments – to upload their data directly? And what about external service providers, such as your market research firm or media agency? What are the access rights? Who needs the privilege to change data and parameters? Who gets to work with the output, and in what way? Do you make selected reports available to your partners outside the marketing department? Answering these questions early on will help you leverage the IT solution to its full potential.

Application examples: Smooth integration versus step change

How do you embed an IT-enabled marketing ROI solution in marketing operations? Here are two examples we have encountered in our work with clients. While the approaches these companies took were very different, both were ultimately successful through combining the benefits of a tool with the characteristics of their corporate culture and business priorities:

- A leading retailer chose to integrate the output of the new solution with existing processes. The company was already working with dashboards and regular reviews of marketing KPIs as a matter of course. Instead of introducing new formats, the company adapted existing dashboards and reports to reflect the KPIs produced by the new tool. Because the output was brought to them in a familiar format, executives quickly adopted the new metrics and starting using them in their decision making. In similar spirit, the company did not set up dedicated training sessions. Instead, the IT solution was added to the agenda of the standard new hire orientation as well as to the training curriculum for existing employees. The tool became a part of daily operations with minimal disruption to existing processes.

- Another company – a global consumer goods manufacturer – took the opposite approach. They used the IT solution to trigger a mindset change across the entire organization. Since the company's approach was characterized by tradition and routine, the CMO used the tool to overcome organizational inertia and foster more experimentation. Based on scenario modelling, the marketing team simulated the effects of new marketing vehicles, tested them in a random set of pilot markets, and fed the results back into the tool. Incremental profit exceeded even the most optimistic scenario, and an adjusted marketing mix was quickly rolled out to other markets. Before long, the company had evolved from an old-school advertiser into a marketing innovator.

Note that there is a broad range of service providers with different focus areas. Examples include Market Share and Tableau in marketing operations, Google Analytics and Visual IQ in middle ware, Accenture, SAP, and SAS in backbone platforms, and IBM, Oracle, and Adobe in infrastructure.

Once the tool and the relevant protocols are in place, use the metrics and the analyses it provides as often as possible in daily operations. Refer to the lessons learned from past planning cycles, and use scenario modelling to expand the fact base for future decisions. Make sure the marketing-ROI-related KPIs produced by the tool are included in corporate performance reviews, and don't hesitate to use visuals exported from a marketing ROI solution on your intranet site, in newsletters, and in presentations to stakeholders. Before you know it, IT-enabled marketing ROI optimization will be second nature to your team, and your executive peers will approach you to discuss the results or conduct additional analyses. Don't be put off if they challenge the output. In fact, encourage them to do more of it. There is no such thing as a fool-proof solution, and even the finest tool will be more effective in the hands of an experienced practitioner. Over time, you will find yourself building a growing and ever more sophisticated "technology stack" of multiple marketing ROI solutions, hand-picked and updated to support all of your key marketing decisions.

Key takeaways

- Take stock of the vendor landscape. Get a sense of what is out there, but think about what you need before you commit yourself to a specific provider or application.
- Define realistic requirements. Talk to your team before you talk to prospective vendors. Simplicity and ease of use help ensure people actually use the tool.
- Get the ball rolling. Engage your peers, your team, and early users of an IT solution as in-house advocates of fact-based marketing throughout your company.
- Create a legacy. Actively manage the way the tool is used and maintained. Use the output to trigger discussions about what's best for your brand.

NOTES

1. http://www.gartner.com/newsroom/id/2833517 (retrieved November 2015).
2. Robert Lee Hotz, "Mars probe lost due to simple math error," *Los Angeles Times*, October 1, 1999; http://articles.latimes.com/1999/oct/01/news/mn-17288.
3. Same-store sales are defined as sales generated by those stores that have been open more than a year, so that the company has historical data to compare current sales with sales generated during the same period in the previous year.
4. http://www.mckinsey.com/client_service/marketing_and_sales/tools_and_solutions/the_marketing_navigator.
5. http://www.forbes.com/sites/ilyapozin/2013/07/28/15-marketing-softwares-that-can-boost-your-business/.

10 – AGILITY

Infuse your organization with a return on investment mindset

Why does agility matter?

Have you been keeping track of the goods we are dishing out? Multi-lens budget sizing. Granular allocation. Insights-driven messaging. Creative storytelling. Like-for-like instrument comparisons. Advanced mix modelling. Smart activation. Superior systems and solutions. Trust-based performance partnerships. With a toolbox like that, how can you go wrong? Actually, it's all for nothing unless you make sure these fine tools are put to good use. For sustained impact, marketers need to use these tools not once, but continuously. The new, evidence-based approach to marketing performance management we have outlined in the preceding nine chapters depends upon you to invest in the capabilities of your team and change the way you work.

Think back to what you have read and ask yourself: Do I have the right people to do the required research, oversee the necessary analyses, draw the right inferences, and take appropriate action? Is there someone on my team who can build and maintain the technological infrastructure that will support data-driven decision making across the organization? Are our processes and decision rules set up to absorb the new insights, align our activities, monitor the impact, and make real-time adjustments to the marketing plan? No?

Don't worry. Very few CMOs will say "yes" to all of these questions. It's not a checklist anyway. The important point is to realize that change will only happen if you make it happen.

Tools are great. But – mathematically speaking – a great toolbox is just a necessary, not a sufficient, condition of optimal marketing performance. To reap the full benefit of fact-based marketing performance management, you need to upgrade your organization in two other respects as well: people and processes. Even the most comprehensive database, the finest software solutions, and the most sophisticated analyses will go to waste unless you have the people who can make sense of the results, and the processes to ensure that these results shape everyday decisions. According to a recent McKinsey study, good processes give you 1.5 times the ROI increase generated by good analytics alone (Exhibit 10.1).[1] What's more, companies that invest in marketing capabilities consistently outperform their peers. According to a global benchmarking study, revenue growth at companies with advanced marketing and sales capabilities exceeds the sector average by 30 percent (Exhibit 10.2).[2]

Marketing can do much more than advertise a finished product to the public. Best-practice marketing actively shapes a company's face

Decisions rated on quality of analysis and process by survey respondents (n = 728)

	Quality of process →	
Quality of data/analysis ↑	Good analysis but poor process 19%	Good analysis and good process 32%
	Poor analysis and poor process 17%	Good process but poor analysis 30%

Exhibit 10.1   Average return on investment.
Source: McKinsey

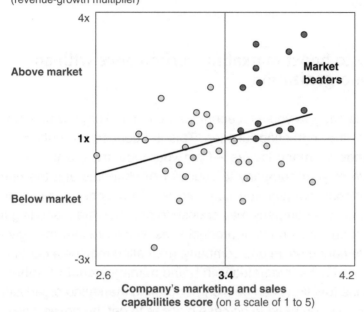

Company's performance
(revenue-growth multiplier)

Exhibit 10.2 Correlation of performance and capabilities.
Source: McKinsey analysis

to its customers, spanning multiple functions and all touch points. To maximize customer value, marketing needs to get involved in proposition development from the earliest stages of the value chain. Even if ideation, research, and development are invisible to the customer, the outcome of these processes has a huge impact on the customer's ultimate experience. In customer-centric organizations, all functions look to the CMO for guidance on how to drive customer value – with the right products, relevant features, competitive prices, convenient channels, and superior service. Communication will remain an important part of marketing, both with respect to the brand promise and the specific benefits of a given product or service, but it will only be one of several aspects of how marketing infuses companies with the customer understanding they need in order to prosper.

How to boost marketing performance with an agile organization

We will not give you a blueprint for the optimal organizational structure of the marketing function. This is because the right structure depends on many factors – from your industry and the corporate culture of your company to your mix of channels and the number of national markets you compete in. Even under similar circumstances, one company may choose to organize the marketing function by business units or product lines, while another may give priority to countries. In one company, marketing may be a central unit, while it may be integrated with brand management in another. And all these functions can be high-performing marketing organizations. Ultimately, you need to go case by case to get the boxes, lines, and decision rules right for any given company.

In this chapter, we will focus on five success factors that we have seen at work in high-performing, modern marketing organizations: speed, simplicity, substance, story, and science.[3] While not all aspects are equally important for all types of organizations, every company should aspire to build robust skills in each of them.[4] Think of these five characteristics as criteria you can use to check whether your organization is ready for the new, golden age of marketing as an agile, data-driven hub of customer centricity that drives return on investment and overall company performance.

Speed: Increase the clock rate of your team, but slow down if the stakes are high

Marketing was once a slow-paced function. Service provider contracts were reviewed every few years, if at all. Campaign planning and media buying were done a year in advance. Impact was evaluated on a quarterly basis at best. At the most aggregated level, it will stay this way, if only because the company as a whole runs on these cycles. But the pace of operational marketing is quickening. The lead time from ideation to execution is decreasing, as is the delay between stimuli and response. Your messages reach your audience more quickly than ever before, information on consumer reactions and marketing impact becomes increasingly available in real time, and your competitors react more swiftly to changing conditions. Sitting and waiting was never a sustainable stance for marketers. Today, it is a form of neglect that markets will neither forgive nor forget.

Acceleration is in evidence across the entire spectrum of instruments, but it is most dramatic in digital marketing (see Chapter 6). Users expect you to enter into a continuous dialogue with them. They have no patience to wait days or weeks for your answers to their questions, your reactions to their ideas, and your resolution of their concerns. To master the digital dialogue, you have to ramp up your capabilities in two respects. First, become more receptive to the signals customers are sending. The signal can be as clear as a customer clicking on a link you have placed in a newsletter or an ad, but it can also be harder to pick up. For example, it takes systematic efforts and dedicated software solutions to track the topics – and gauge the sentiment – of conversations about your company in social media. Second, you need to become more responsive to such signals and get back to customers with appropriate reactions as quickly as possible. Nestlé, for example, has established a digital acceleration programme to train marketers from all parts of the organization in the arts of social media listening and real-time interaction with customers, enabled by substantial investments in technology.[5]

Of course, speed isn't equally important in all areas of marketing and at all levels of your organization. We encourage you to try out new ways of working in central marketing – or in a test market – to get rapid feedback on the impact, and roll out the things that are proven to work to business units and countries. "Speed comes from local autonomy to take local action," says the CMO at a leading consumer goods company. As you set out to accelerate your organization, differentiate between three types of decisions[6] and adjust your speed accordingly:

- Frequent, tactical decisions that are part of a continuous process – such as online ad buying, media auditing, or managing online customer dialogues – for which fast responses are crucial to drive customer satisfaction. Use a formal approach – such as RACI codes (responsible, accountable, consult, inform) – to clarify decision responsibility, set up clear protocols, and conduct a dry run before you go live.
- Periodic decisions with strategic implications – such as budget sizing, changes to the instrument mix, or sign-off on major campaigns. For these decisions, you need to balance speed and flexibility with the need for a reliable fact base and correct inferences. Make sure you have repeated, collaborative interactions with key stakeholders – such as the CFO, product managers, and general managers of national subsidiaries – before you make a decision.
- High-stakes decisions with long-term effects – such as hiring a new senior executive, repositioning an important brand in your portfolio, or selecting a new lead agency. Think of these as Jefferson decisions. "Delay is preferable to error," Thomas Jefferson said about high-stakes decisions in a letter to George Washington. Take your time, take precautions against prejudice, and take counsel with independent experts – such as an executive search consultancy, a strategic marketing consulting firm, or a pitch management agency.

Automation is a key enabler of agility, but it isn't everything. Agility is driven by mindset at least as much as it is driven by processes and protocols. Start accelerating the mental clock speed of the marketing team by introducing a more flexible campaign calendar. Make detailed plans only for major campaigns, but leave wiggle room for smaller, more tactical activities. Meet with your team on a weekly basis to agree on priorities. Encourage your direct reports to conduct daily stand-up meetings with their teams for progress reviews and real-time refinements. Have them run frequent live pilots to instill a sense of achievement in the organization. At the same time, educate your service providers to supply you with impact data more quickly, and make them your partners in a process of continuous improvement. Last but not least, don't hesitate to kill the things that don't work: tools that create more extra work than benefits (see Chapter 9), campaigns that fail to reach predefined objectives (see Chapters 1 to 3), and instruments that don't live up to your standards in terms of reach, cost, and quality (see Chapter 5).

Simplicity: Learn to walk before you run; create a culture of testing and learning in which failure is accepted

You may be tempted to implement everything you have read about in this book all at once, and to go all the way right away: city-level growth planning, segment-specific purchase driver analysis, award-winning storytelling, advanced single-user attribution modelling. We have one word of advice for you: don't. Instead, take things one step at a time. There is no point in buying expensive software if your organization is not equipped to use the output it produces for better decision making. Put yourself in the shoes of line managers in your organization. How can you make their lives easier, rather than creating extra work for them? In the real world, a clean-cut dashboard app that brings key marketing performance indicators to the smart phones of every executive can make a bigger difference than a high-end marketing ROI solution suite. Aspire to spare frontline staff the complexity of gathering information from diverse sources, cleaning up the database, and performing advanced analysis. Instead, give them what they need to make better decisions: up-to-date campaign impact figures, improvement ideas for their local marketing mix, or a typing tool that helps them tailor their propositions to customer needs.

One leading pharmaceuticals company, for example, has equipped its entire sales force with a tablet-based pitch tool. Prior to meeting with a physician or a hospital's representative, the sales rep answers a set of simple questions about who they are about to see – such as their area of focus, typical order volume, and willingness to try out new types of treatment. Based on the answers, the tool suggests an appropriate sales script, a preselection of recommended products, and a sliding scale of price discounts. In the background, all kinds of big data, market research, and advanced analytics are at work: a database of past transactions, needs-based segmentation analysis, competitive pricing intelligence, and dynamic sensitivity analysis. But all that is invisible to sales reps. They only see what they need to see to do a better job. As a result, the tool enjoys the highest acceptance rates the company has ever seen for a new piece of software, and sales force effectiveness has soared since its introduction.

Digital marketing is particularly susceptible to overly complex approaches, simply because so much data is available and even the most outlandish analyses can be performed at the push of a button. But often, simple improvements are more effective drivers of marketing performance than sophisticated systems. Start by having your team monitor the impact of their activities systematically and act on the insights this generates. If personalized outbound e-mail campaigning resonates well with your customers, do more of it, even if it seems old-fashioned and self-appointed gurus suggest premium rich media ads instead. Empower your team to test, track, and learn. Make it clear that failure is accepted – as long as people learn from their mistakes. A simple way to foster a spirit of experimentation is a controlled environment, such as vinoya.eu, an online wine store that is part of McKinsey's Capability Centre.[7] During hands-on training sessions, executives take over vinoya.eu for a limited time. Participants get to experience firsthand how their decisions influence shopper behaviour, and they feel a real rush from experiencing cause and effect live. The specific success factors of online marketing may differ from industry to industry, but most managers are thrilled at the prospect of transferring what they have learned in a protected environment to their own businesses.

In many companies, real-time improvements to running campaigns may require collaboration across functional silos and outside standard reporting lines. "We need help to get through this jungle," says the CMO at a consumer goods company. But before you make structural changes, hire a few new people with relevant experience, assemble a cross-functional team, and provide them with a test budget. Before long, you will see whether the new approach produces the desired results – more efficient customer acquisition, higher brand recognition, or better repurchase rates. If it does, roll it out. One telecommunications company, for instance, realized that its complex organizational structure was getting in the way of delivering top-notch customer service. The company created a unit that combined existing call centres and a newly formed social media customer care group. The leader of the unit reports directly to the board. Proximity to the top of the company allows the new team to collaborate more smoothly across the organization. At the same time, the new setup signals to the organization that a seamless customer experience is a top priority for the company.[8]

Substance: Unleash the power of marketing on the guts of your business to create a satisfying end-to-end experience for customers

"It's not a bug, it's a feature." The line may have originated as a joke among 1980s software developers, but it is indicative of a particular understanding of marketing that still prevails in many engineering-driven companies today. In this view, marketing is little more than an appendix to product development. If the product doesn't live up to expectations, marketers will charm customers into buying it anyway with sweet little lies. In the past, companies might have gotten away with such sugarcoating. Today, there is no more tolerance for fluffy talk – let alone downright deceptive messages. Heartened by consumer advocacy and class action suits for compensation, consumers are more vocal than ever about what they like – and especially, what they do not like. Thanks to social media, disappointment spreads more quickly than in the past, and embellished claims about product benefits can seriously harm a company's financial performance.

But even if things don't go wrong in a big way, companies that treat marketing as an afterthought often miss out on substantial value creation opportunities. One car manufacturer, for example, did not involve the marketing department in the development of a new minivan until just before its launch. As a result, the new model came with all kinds of innovations nobody cared about – such as an adaptive rear axle – while it lacked some crucial features – such as adjustable rear seats for a flexible interior setup. To make things worse, all the innovative engineering had made the car too expensive for many young families, its main target group. This was a clear case of marketing coming too late. But premature marketing is no better. One offline player under pressure from pure online players, for example, ran a large-scale media campaign focusing on "real-time service," but failed to invest in actual process streamlining. By focusing solely on messaging without bringing the substance of the business in line, the company effectively broke its promise to consumers. The story spread quickly in social media and was eventually picked up by mainstream media. It took years for the company to recover from the resulting damage to its reputation and its business.

We believe that good marketing is truly consequential. CMOs today can create real value if they venture to shape the substance of the business: product features, service interactions, the entire customer experience. Armed with information about customers' needs and their relation with the company, the CMO is in a unique position to help other functions improve their offering, increase customer satisfaction, and create sustainable value. If the substance is flawed, even the finest communication will go to waste. But if the substance reflects what you know about customer needs, communication will be much more effective. If you infuse the entire business system with marketing expertise, everybody wins: product managers, marketers, customers, and the company as a whole.

One energy provider, for example, decided to differentiate its brand and justify its price premium by promising the best service in the industry. But before they went public with the promise, the company used customer insights to conduct an end-to-end overhaul of the customer experience. The programme spanned all major milestones, from onboarding and billing to moving house and changing tariffs. Among other things, the company found through market research that customers were discouraged from switching providers because they found the onboarding process too cumbersome – lots of paperwork, phone calls to different departments, repeated appointments for manual meter readings, and so on. In response, the company went to great lengths to simplify core processes dramatically and move large parts of the customer interaction to a new online platform, backed by a unified IT system that spares customers and service agents the hassle of having to enter the same information again and again. Marketing also took the lead in an effort to create new products. The CMO led a cross-functional team of sales, IT, and product development managers to develop a smart thermostat that would help consumers conserve energy. The company was richly rewarded for this comprehensive, customer-centric transformation effort. It now enjoys the highest level of brand preference in the industry, a growing customer base, and above-average loyalty in a fiercely competitive industry plagued by growing churn rates.

Such efforts are extending the reach of marketing into the guts of the business. As the CMO, you are well placed to help your organization detect and meet customer expectations. You know what customers care about, how much they are willing to pay for it, what bugs them, and what drives their loyalty. We encourage you to take advantage of this opportunity to help your company create more attractive products, more satisfying service interactions, and a consistent, seamless overall experience that reflects the values of your brand.

Improving the customer's experience end to end

Is the customer at the centre of your company's processes? Are all relevant departments – marketing, research, CRM, sales, store management, aftersales support, IT, accounting – working in synch to provide customers with a seamless experience? Here are some questions to pressure-test the customer centricity of your processes:

- *Minimal efforts?* Are you doing everything you can to make things as easy as possible for your customers? Can you reduce the number of steps required to complete a task, such as the number of clicks or personal interactions?
- *Seamless integration?* Is your organization equipped to pick up a process that originated in one channel in another channel at a later stage? Is all relevant information shared between departments to avoid double entries and conflicting data?
- *Personalization?* Do customers have the freedom to choose their own journey? Do your systems recognize individuals and provide them with content and options that reflect their personal preferences?
- *Transparency?* Is it clear to customers from the beginning what to expect in terms of process steps, timing, and data they will need to supply? Is all relevant information easily available?

- *Pleasant experience?* Will customers remember the interaction with your company as a pleasant experience? Are your personnel friendly, well-trained, and accommodating?

Start with a simple diagnostic to pinpoint your strengths and weaknesses. Conduct root cause analysis in areas of apparent weakness. Make targeted improvements in these areas. Build on these improvements as you work towards a superior end-to-end experience.

Story: Reinvent the marketing department as a newsroom and engage consumers as co-creators of brand-related content

Storytelling is a great way for companies to cut through the clutter of competitive communication and engage with consumers on an emotional level (see Chapter 4). But it also makes new demands on the marketing organization. You need to adopt a publisher's mindset, you need to hire and develop a new breed of people, and you need to set up at least part of the marketing department as a newsroom. In the past, a punchline for a new campaign every couple of months may have done the trick. In the future, you need to keep the cliffhangers coming every other day. Note, however, that such real-time storytelling approaches make new demands not only on the marketing department, but also require different, more flexible support models from legal and compliance. There are two basic archetypes of systematic content creation we observe in our work with leading marketers worldwide:

- Multiplatform content creators. These companies develop their own stories for activation at multiple touch points – from TV ads and YouTube clips to print ads and POS materials.
- Online content aggregators. These companies provide a forum for customers and experts to review products, report on experiences, and engage in discussions or co-creation efforts.

Leading personal care companies, for example, have assembled cross-functional teams that develop online tools to match products to skin types, produce makeup tutorials for dissemination on YouTube, and provide live customer advice. Some of these players also venture into the content aggregation space, e.g., by encouraging consumers to counsel each other on the company's website. Examples of pure content aggregation include travel portals like Expedia and TripAdvisor, which provide a forum for users to review hotels and describe travel destinations, but reserve the right to select and edit consumer contributions to fit the overall narrative of their brands as independent brokers. For online retailers like Amazon, user reviews of books and movies are a big deal. In 2013, Amazon acquired goodreads.com, a user-populated database of books, annotations, and reviews that has since been cross-linked with Amazon's retail business to enrich the user experience and provide an additional incentive for readers to explore and buy new books.[9]

Science: Infuse the marketing team with a spirit of systematic experimentation and fact-based optimization

There's often a perceived conflict between art and science in marketing. We don't see it this way. Marketing needs both art and science to succeed. Of course, science can mean advanced analytics, sophisticated regression modeling, and automated algorithms for auction-based media buying (see Chapter 6). More fundamentally, though, science is about forming a hypothesis, conducting an experiment, and observing what happens to validate, refute, or refine the hypothesis. This is exactly the approach – and the mindset – modern marketing needs. Direct marketers have done it for a long time: send mailing A to one group of customers, send mailing B to another group of customers, see which one generates more responses, and then run with the winner on a larger scale. Scientific marketing is about making a habit of this practice – across campaigns, target groups, and instruments. Put an end to hit and miss. Instead, test and learn. Whatever you do, clarify your intention, record your ingoing assumptions, track the impact, and incorporate the lessons learned into future activities. The challenge is to do it comprehensively and systematically. The good news is that the fact base is growing. Thanks to the rise of targeted digital instruments, a growing share of the budget can be tied to detailed impact figures and submitted to scientific optimization. "The beauty of marketing today is that we can really show the return. The data allows us to demonstrate impact in a much more transparent way than in the past," says Google's CMO Lorraine Twohill.[10]

A leading European communications provider – a former state-owned monopolist – has implemented scientific marketing on a grand scale. It all started with the CMO's frustration about the disconnect between marketing action and consumer reaction. Because of the company's byzantine bureaucracy, it took months to sign off on a new campaign, a new rate structure, or a new service model. Then more months went by while the company called for bids from dozens of service providers in several countries. More than a year elapsed before any new idea actually hit the market, and new propositions had often become obsolete when they finally reached consumers. In the meantime, many other things had happened in the market – changes in regulation, competitor moves, new market entrants going live with virtual operator brands. As a result, it was impossible to connect market impact to marketing activities and learn from experience. To change this, the CMO set up a marketing lab, but not as most people know it. In this case, the lab was an entire country, although a small one on Europe's eastern fringes. With a small team of like-minded people and a network of trusted providers, the CMO developed a system of rapid prototyping, live market tests, and real-time adjustments to running campaigns and new rate structures. When she finally went to the board with a new proposal, it would be backed by detailed reports on how it had affected the test market in terms of customer acquisition, retention, average revenue per user, brand equity, and other KPIs. She has never had to endure lengthy discussions and cumbersome clearance processes again.

Good marketing is and will remain a combination of art, craft, and science. It has always been, and will always be, about art. The craft, though, has changed with more touch points, and the science has changed with more data. Millions of customers are interacting with companies, and with each other, at dozens of touch points, leaving a trail of terabytes of data. Retailers are under pressure to manage thousands of price points and hundreds of promotions in real time across multiple channels. Increasingly, machines are talking to machines as price comparison portals are taking hold and automated ad auctions are getting more common. Without science, you will be lost. This is why we encourage you to expand the analytical skill set of your team. Hire and develop marketing analysts who are comfortable handling large amounts of data, looking for patterns, and deriving inferences from their observations. Also, hire marketing technology experts who will help you bridge the gap between strategy and operations. Then have the new guys mingle with veteran marketers to make sure marketing is infused with science, and science with customer understanding. Some CEOs we know believe it's time to create a new position rooted both in technology and marketing, the marketing technology officer (MTO) – someone who knows what can be automated, when judgement is required, and where to seek out and place new technical talent. But even the MTO may leave your company eventually. This is why you also need to invest in tools and systems that embed evidence-based decision making in your business system (see Exhibit 10.3 for an example and Chapter 9 for details).

In essence, scientific marketing is nothing but gathering evidence to make better decisions – systematically, continuously, and with an

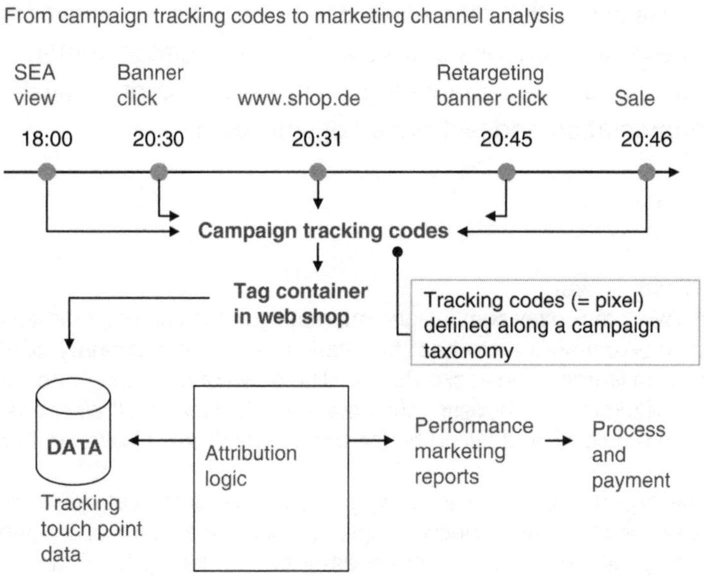

From campaign tracking codes to marketing channel analysis

Exhibit 10.3 Use of tracking codes for performance monitoring (example).
Source: Press search, company information

eye to return on investment. For marketers, science is an opportunity, not a threat. Embrace it, and your company will prosper.

Key takeaways

- Speed. Increase the clock rate of your team, but slow down if the stakes are high.
- Simplicity. Learn to walk before you run; create a culture of testing and learning in which failure is accepted.
- Substance. Unleash the power of marketing on the guts of your business to create a satisfying end-to-end experience for customers.

- Story. Reinvent the marketing department as a newsroom and engage consumers as co-creators of brand-related content.
- Science. Infuse the marketing team with a spirit of systematic experimentation and fact-based optimization.

NOTES

1. McKinsey survey.
2. http://www.mckinsey.com/insights/marketing_sales/building_marketing_and_sales_capabilities_to_beat_the_market (retrieved in January 2016).
3. Jonathan Gordon and Jesko Perrey, "The dawn of marketing's new golden age – Marketers are boosting their precision, broadening their scope, moving more quickly, and telling better stories", *McKinsey Quarterly*, February 2015.
4. Some experts refer to "skill" as a sixth success factor, but skill really cuts across the other five. Speed, simplicity, substance, story, and science all make specific demands on the skills of the marketing team, and we will discuss these requirements in the respective sections.
5. https://www.youtube.com/watch?v=ktsMa8hfgY0 (retrieved in January 2016).
6. Based on *What are the big ideas? Decision making and organizational design*, McKinsey publication.
7. http://capability-center.mckinsey.com/.
8. Jonathan Gordon and Jesko Perrey, "The dawn of marketing's new golden age – Marketers are boosting their precision, broadening their scope, moving more quickly, and telling better stories", *McKinsey Quarterly*, February 2015.
9. http://www.theguardian.com/books/2013/apr/02/amazon-purchase-goodreads-stuns-book-industry (retrieved in January 2016).
10. http://www.mckinsey.com/insights/marketing_sales/how_google_breaks_through (retrieved in January 2016).

CREDITS

Contributors

Sebastian Ackermann
Benjamin Brudler
Lars Fiedler
Carmen Gayoso
Marco Guida
Jan Hildebrand
Jeff Jacobs
Sascha Lehmann
Nils Liedtke
David Ochmann
Philip C. Ogren
Julia Rath
Marleen Relling
Katharina Siorpaes
Jeremy Urban
Hiek Van der Scheer
Lorenz Zimmermann

Production team
Rik Kirkland
Alice Kral
Scott Reznik
Sanya van Schalkwyk
Kinga Young

Executive editor
Cornelius Grupen

INDEX